The Men who would be King

To Renée van der Vloodt

The Men who would be King

A Look at Royalty in Exile

NICHOLAS SHAKESPEARE

SIDGWICK & JACKSON

LONDON

First published in Great Britain in 1984
by Sidgwick & Jackson Limited

Copyright © 1984 Nicholas Shakespeare
Preface copyright © 1984 Anthony Holden Ltd

Picture research by Philippa Lewis

ISBN 0-283-98948-3

Phototypeset by Falcon Graphic Art Ltd
Wallington, Surrey
Printed in Great Britain by
Biddles Ltd, Guildford, Surrey
for Sidgwick & Jackson Limited
1 Tavistock Chambers, Bloomsbury Way
London WC1A 2SG

Contents

Acknowledgements

To some extent this book grew out of my research while setting up the BBC documentary of the same name. I am grateful to the BBC – in particular to Roger Laughton, Head of Network Features – for letting me take time off to write it, and for permission to use material from the programme.

A newcomer to the royal scene – worse still, a loiterer – I am indebted to the works of people far more qualified than I. Among them, *The Uneasy Heads* by Geoffrey Bocca, *Royalty in Exile* by Charles Fenyvesi, *The Bourbon Kings of France* by Desmond Seward, *Napoleon III and Eugénie* by Jasper Ridley, *Lupescu* by Alice Leone Moats, *Il Re Dall'Esilio* edited by Falcone Lucifero, *The Fall of the House of Savoy* by Robert Katz, *From Caesar to the Mafia* by Luigi Barzini, *The Last Habsburg* by Gordon Brook Shepherd, *The Rebel Prince* by Louis Ferdinand Hohenzollern, *The File on the Tsar* by A. Summers and T. Mangold, *Anastasia* by Peter Kurth, *Histoire du Royaume D'Araucanie* by Philippe, Prince d'Araucanie and *Kings Over the Water* by Theo Aronson – not forgetting the journals of the Monarchist League, the Monarchist Press Association and the Twickenham Local History Society. (There is a full Bibliography at the back of the book.)

Those who gave me information and assistance of every kind are too numerous to name here. They know who they are and my heartfelt thanks to them all. It would, nevertheless, be remiss of me to make no special mention of Cleveland Amory, Michael Bloch, Mark Bonham Carter, Bruce Chatwin, Margaret and Pam Davis, Lord Eccles, Mary Espirito Santo, Norman Field, Anthony Holden, Libby Joy, the late Hester Marsden-Smedley, Charles Miller, Hugh Montgomery-Massingberd,

George Plumptre, Judith Symington, D.W. Thompson Vessey, Count Nikolai Tolstoy, Monique Udureanu, Hugo Vickers, Gore Vidal, Renée van der Vloodt, David Williamson and Michael Wynne-Parker.

Finally, to those who form the subject of this book, my gratitude for their courtesy, help and unfailing generosity.

List of Illustrations

'Sad, like Kings in their photographs.'
LOUIS ARAGON

Preface

'Fronting' a television documentary is neither as easy nor as difficult as it looks. There's a lot to worry about: how your hair is looking; whether you're wearing the same tie as yesterday; whether you can say fifty words to camera without forgetting or tripping over them. The least of your worries, mercifully, is having to know what you're talking about. All that is done for you.

As you fly to exotic locations like Portugal at the BBC's expense, you mug up on today's interviewee in documents compiled by a researcher. By the time you get round to writing the script, he or she has taught you everything you need to know. In my case, when making the BBC-TV documentary *The Men who would be King*, that researcher was Nicholas Shakespeare.

When the job of presenting the film was first offered to me, in the spring of 1982, I had my doubts. Newly and somewhat unexpectedly unemployed, I needed the work. But I had spent the last four years, since writing a biography of Prince Charles, trying to avoid being typecast as a royal specialist. I had worked as a Washington correspondent and a features editor, boldly turning away countless commissions to write and broadcast about the royals. Riveting though they are, there are other things in life.

What's more, I had taken on various commitments which were going to limit my time. Beggars can't be too choosy, I told the director, Charles Miller, but I feared I didn't have much time to rummage around in the pasts of sundry exiled monarchs. No problem, said Miller. Shakespeare, his assistant producer, had already done it.

Those who have met Nicholas Shakespeare will be familiar with his inexhaustible supply of charm. It exudes from the pages that follow. Without it, I suspect, that film could not have been made, nor this book written. Apart from anything else, it opens doors. I first experienced its effects within seconds of meeting him to plan the filming. In the most beguiling way, he made it perfectly clear that I shouldn't start wondering whether to write a book about all this. He himself, I was to understand, had the matter well in hand. When I switched on my own brand of charm, saying I was mightily relieved, and wishing him well with his project, Nicholas didn't look too convinced. The more I got into the subject, the more I understood why. It's a marvellous theme for a book. And a fifty-minute TV documentary could do but scant justice to his voluminous research.

So it is with pride in throat that I now commend the job he has done. As we travelled Europe 'collecting' our ex- and would-be Kings, Nicholas became an evangelist for the cause. His enthusiasm for netting and mounting these rare specimens, many of them pretty elusive, was both exhausting and infectious.

Seville offered a highlight. While I prided myself on cornering the King of Spain at a cocktail party, hoping Nicholas was watching with envy, that charm was at work across the room, arranging to spend its owner's summer holidays as a house-guest of the Countess of Paris. Her niece, what's more, seemed to be promoting his cause with some vigour. Shakespeare had done it again.

It would be too easy to mock exiled royalty, whose pretensions often belie the real world. Nicholas Shakespeare's account of them is good-humoured, and gives credit where it's due. Were it not, for instance, for Otto von Habsburg, Austria might well now be a Soviet satellite state.

Some of these people have used their positions to make a little bit of history. Some, like Prince Nicholas Romanoff and King Rechad, were ready to laugh with us at their unenviable lot. Others, who had suffered more, exuded poignancy: we were both affected by our meeting with King Umberto of Italy, so shortly before his death. In Alexander of Yugoslavia we both made a friend – an impressive man much our own age, solemnly prepared for some quirk of fate to change his life, but entirely realistic about the long odds against it. Prince Louis-Ferdinand Hohenzollern was as eager to play us his piano compositions as to talk about his chances of restoration under Hitler. The Duke of Bragança inquired anxiously about potential English brides.

All the members of this curious club, in their diverse ways, lead rather forlorn lives, and were happy to enjoy a fleeting moment of celebrity. Several wrote to me in high excitement after seeing the film. It had, they felt, done them justice. I, for my part, feel that is even truer of this book.

Anthony Holden

Introduction: 'We the Gods'

'I'm a King without a job and the only job I know is how to be a King.'
                                            KING PETER OF YUGOSLAVIA
                                                          •

One morning in the heart of Montparnasse, I was given lunch by a small precise man with a grey herring-bone moustache and eyes inflamed by glaucoma. His name was Philippe Boiry and he ran a public relations firm in the Faubourg Poissonnière, and a faculty of law in Notre Dame des Champs.

'Do you know the reason for the "royal we"?', he asked, filling a briar pipe. 'It goes back to the Roman Emperors who thought they were deities. When they spoke they began with the phrase, "We the gods".'

Later, engulfed in smoke, he quoted Machiavelli. '*Qui veut gouverner les hommes doit se dire issu de Dieu.*'

God has rather forsaken Monsieur Boiry. As the hereditary Prince of Araucania and Patagonia he is heir to a kingdom five times the size of France, a kingdom, incidentally, that includes the Falkland Islands. His first visit to South America was to be later that autumn, by courtesy of Chilean Television. He was looking forward to going. It would be the first time a member of the Royal House of Araucania had been back since a brief period of rule in the nineteenth century.

Sovereigns have always styled themselves as representatives of God. The Emperor of Austria was known as His Apostolic Majesty; the King of France, His Christian Majesty; of Portugal, Fidelissimo; of Spain, His Catholic Majesty. Today our own Queen remains Defender of the Faith.

Fifteen years ago an opinion poll taken in Britain showed that a third of the population had reason to believe Elizabeth II was chosen by God. The King of Nepal is officially a son of the Almighty. Though he is an Old Etonian, he would not consider his divine right a matter for serious discussion; nor would the Emperor of Japan refer to his descent from Amaterasu, the sun goddess raped by her brother, Susanoo, the god of lust.

This century has somewhat cropped the divinity that used to hedge a king. Today his touch is just as likely to transmit scrofula as to cure it for we know now that all of us are made of the same clay. (Also that, like cream jugs and chamber pots, we tend to get used for different purposes.) Not even a monarch is immune from what might be called the realities of modern life. 'There's a lot of unemployment in my profession,' Albert I of the Belgians once said, and royal redundancies have been especially bad in recent years. Two world wars claimed the thrones of four emperors and eleven kings, demonstrating that their powers derived more from the will of the people than from the grace of God. According to the corpulent King Farouk, there will only be five monarchs left in Europe by the year 2000: the four kings in a pack of cards and the King of England.

In power, it is in a king's interest to promote, and inhabit, the popular fairy-tale existence. One Spanish Queen refused a gift of silk stockings because it was not thought wise for her people to know she had legs. Perhaps for this reason, a sovereign tends to pick his mistress from a similar world of make-believe: the stage. Leading men and ladies include Ludwig I of Bavaria and the dancer Lola Montez; Franz Josef of Austria and the actress Katharina Schratt; Tsar Nicholas II and the ballerina Matilda Kschessinska; and Manoel II of Portugal and the French dancer Gaby Deslys. With the advent of picture palaces and the movie screen, royal focus shifted to Hollywood queens. King Umberto of Italy paid court to Jeanette Macdonald and Dolores del Rio; Louis Ferdinand of Prussia contemplated a life with Lili Damita. Prince Rainier of Monaco married Grace Kelly.

Until the midnight hour these men and women had been kept from the public eye in their ivory towers. Once their carriages changed into pumpkins, they proved to possess a great deal of human nature. Ex-kings showed they not only had legs, but were also rather unsteady on them. Deprived of their thrones many continued to live as play-actors; they disguised themselves with dark glasses and false whiskers and adopted names like Mr Brown, Mr Jones and Jean Prat. Their careers are, nevertheless, romantic. Ernest Hemingway used the King of Spain's father, the Count of Barcelona, as a model for one of his heroes, while King Peter of

Yugoslavia claimed his own tale 'in so many ways outstrips fiction'.

If the flight of kings gave rise to yet more legends, it was also a relatively bloodless operation. A king, however unattractive his character, was, through his dynasty, the embodiment of history and tradition. He was the living flag of his nation, and, as Shakespeare illustrated – 'Our brother France', 'bloody England' – he bore its name. As such he was protected by sufficient divinity to escape with his life. With the exception of Tsar Nicholas II, a twentieth-century monarch rarely suffered the justice meted out to short-term leaders such as Mussolini and Robespierre. In several cases, had he been willing to shed blood like them, and like them involve himself in politics, he may not have found it necessary to leave.

Britain played a major hand in the fortunes of deposed monarchs. The Royal Navy lived up to its name in transporting the Lisbon court to Rio in 1808, the last king of Portugal to Britain in 1910, the last emperor of Austria-Hungary to Madeira in 1921, and the last sultan from Turkey in the following year. During the Second World War, this scepter'd isle became a refuge for the royal families of Norway, Denmark, Luxembourg, the Netherlands, Greece, Yugoslavia and Albania – most of whom were descended from Queen Victoria. In their suites at Claridge's and the Ritz, they performed what Churchill called a 'beggar's opera'.

Ironically for a country which is today the symbol of monarchy, Britain was in more ways than one responsible for their arrival. The part she played in dismantling the monarchies of Yugoslavia, Romania, Germany, even Patagonia, is not a noble one.

What happens, though, to men without a throne? Do they and their families take with them into exile a sense of divine right, expecting to be treated like the Caesars as living deities? Or do they share the view of Frederick the Great, that a crown is just a hat that lets the rain in, and that monarchy is like virginity, once lost, gone for ever?

Such questions were prompted by a party I attended in the winter of 1979. My parents, who were living in Lisbon, were invited with their family for drinks at the *quinta* of a retired Englishman. My father had got it into his head that we were the only guests, and our clothes suited the informality of the occasion. Turning off a lane behind the high-rise flats of Cascais, we drove into the *quinta*'s empty courtyard and parked beneath a large illuminated Christmas tree. As we fumbled with our seatbelts, the white doors of the house opened in unison. Two uniformed maids stood aside for the hostess, who appeared on the steps in a voluminous red dress and a collar of pearls. She affected an ecstatic greeting. In contrast to us in our suede shoes and patched pullovers, she seemed ready to take her place at the top of the tree.

'I'm sorry we're so late,' my mother said.

'Oh no, you're not at all,' trilled the woman. 'Come in and meet my grandchildren,' she urged, confirming our impression that this was a family affair – as indeed it proved to be, of sorts.

We passed into a vaulted room with gilded wooden carvings on the ceiling and blue and white tiles along the walls. Three pallid young girls stood near the door in conversation with a pair of inattentive men who turned out to be house guests. One, an advertising man, was in disgrace for having shirked Christmas Mass. His taste in cigars and music – 'Scott Joplin records, very loud' – had not gone down well either. The other turned out to be a Central European who had begun life as a butcher and progressed, so he claimed, to Christ Church, Oxford. For some reason he was proud to have known both Burgess and Maclean, 'though you wouldn't trust either of them to walk your dog,' he confided as he steered me to the far end of the room. I was, it seemed, his long-awaited excuse for an assault on the cocktails and crab dips that covered an enormous table. For a glorious half hour I imagined that this sumptuous spread and the waiters who hovered behind it, apparently glad to be of use, were all for us. Then one or two more guests arrived, soliciting some curious kissing of hands, the odd bended knee – and in me a faint sense of doubt.

As the number grew the waiters became more deferential, and the reason apparent. Within the space of an hour, the room contained an assortment of Europe's deposed royal families.

King Umberto of Italy bobbed his domed head at curtsying women, while his sister, Queen Giovanna, the Queen Mother of Bulgaria, pecked at a canapé. On a sofa the Countess of Paris, the woman who would be Queen of France, talked to the Count of Barcelona, the only man to have been both the son and father of a king of Spain without ever ruling himself. Not a throne's throw away stood the Countess's sister, Princess Teresa – a member of the Brazilian royal family – offering her dewy hand to a line of prostrate Habsburgs, Schönbergs and other members of Europe's aristocracy. They were all dressed in blazers and cavalry twill.

There was a sinister-looking Polish count who raced cars in Los Angeles and played the foreign villain in Kojak movies. On Lisbon television, he told me, he could be seen advertising port. He had brought along his step-sister, a beautiful eighteen-year-old who needed cheering up. Her marriage to a sexagenarian tutor had ended with his death after four months. She introduced me to a pug-nosed German archduke whose grandmother was reputed to live in Byron's house in Venice. I asked if this was true. He stiffened and adjusted his spectacles before answering, 'No, Byron lived in her house in Venice.'

My former companions, the advertising man and the Central European, had disappeared. Ignorant of the bows and scrapes of royal protocol, I retreated to a corner and nursed a strong Bloody Mary. Soon I was joined by another refugee. He had a moustache which he stroked nervously and was reassuringly shabby. I took him for a kindred spirit. He had a farm near the town of Viseu, he told me. Vineyards and olives mostly. Did I know that part of Portugal? I was afraid I didn't. Did he know any of these people? Well, yes. In fact he was related to most of them. Was that so? It was indeed. He was the Duke of Bragança, heir to the throne of Portugal.

Some days later, on making the acquaintance of another expatriate – a retired archivist from the United Nations – I came to realize what solecisms I had been in danger of committing that night. A breezy man in a coloured shirt more suited to the Bahamas, he had lived in the area for several years and become part of its social circuit.

'The Salazar régime was very sympathetic to these people, very sympathetic indeed,' he explained, pouring out a cocktail in his small balcony flat. 'They felt it was good for the area. It's the sort of in thing to do, to live in Estoril and Cascais.' He settled back in a chair facing the sea. 'Countesses, they're ten a penny, but you also have all this ex-royalty browsing about. You're probably interested in the drill of what happens when you meet them?'

I nodded. I felt I needed instruction.

'Well, they do rather cling to some sort of formality. Your hostess will ring you up and she'll say, "Will you come and have dinner on Wednesday at half past eight?" Fine. Then she'll say, "Oh, the King is coming," – and you know it's King Umberto because he's the only King – "so therefore would you come about 8.20." One must never arrive after royalty – never, never, never. It just doesn't happen, that sort of thing. Anyhow, you arrive. There's a slight air of expectancy and everyone is looking at the door. You have your gin and tonic in one hand. Finally the King arrives, everyone gets up and the hostess takes the King by the hand and leads him round and introduces him to everyone. Men of course do a little bow and women do their little curtsy. In addressing him you say Your Majesty and then slip into Sire or Sir – or Ma'am in the case of his sister, the Queen of Bulgaria. Then things go back to normal. In some houses they put the King at the head of the table. Not all: the British Embassy in Lisbon does not give pride of place to ex-monarchs. So anyway, you get to table, conversation normal, and again afterwards your hostess will take you up to the King to speak to him. You can't just breeze up and say, "What did you think of last night's *Dallas*, or Jean Harlow's last film?" This isn't done. And you can't leave unless you have a very, very, very pressing reason. I mean, a telephone call, someone's dying, for instance. Otherwise not, which means if it turns out to be a boring dinner party, you're stuck. It happened the other night and everyone said My God, when, when is she going to leave and we all kept waiting and watching and finally she did.'

The party in Cascais, together with my fascination for the way in which its guests, if not their countries, could still command mystique, was the genesis for this study into the fortunes of former ruling families. It was an idiosyncratic journey, neither authoritative nor exhaustive, since one or two important figures – notably King Constantine of Greece, King Simeon of Bulgaria and the Count of Paris – refused to see me. It led me to several strange places and to the doors of some of the oddest people I have ever met. Kings and queens, by and large, are fairly ordinary folk. Monarchy's most bizarre products are those royalty-watchers who support them and their memory. These are the ones who, on the occasion of a sovereign's death bury his effigy in their garden. They are to be caught gate-crashing the wedding of minor royalty where, identified by the lowness of their bows, they are sometimes mistaken for waiters. They are to be seen at bazaars pointing out a princess with the words, 'Of course, she's not one of the real contenders, being of morganatic descent.' They tell stories about how they once met the Countess of Paris at a party and she said 'Hello'. They are to be found everywhere.

Often handicapped by their supporters, my real quarries were, by contrast, extremely normal. Civilized – most had been spanked by British nannies; educated – two had doctorates; and in outlook, surprisingly democratic. With their fondness for smoking, gardening and moustaches they bore many resemblances to English country gentlemen. Some, who could rely on neither suitcases of gold nor donations from supporters, had been forced on to the job market. They had worked as chicken farmers, insurance executives and factory hands. (Even their children, it seems, were trained to cut their coats according to their cloth. At school in Scotland during the 1950s, the Crown Prince of Montenegro bought a large stock of farthings on the eve of their abolition so that he would have a currency ready for his restoration.) Others had chosen a life of obscurity, usually in Portugal, where, surrounded by miniature courts, they spent their time in remembering better days.

If many viewed their birthright as a burden, all continued to see it as a duty. Unlike presidents, kings were trained from childhood, they argued. (Besides, people prefer ermine to suits.) Monarchy was still a politically viable doctrine, they stressed. It provided stability and continuity, and a nation's need for some reflection of itself, a symbol both untouchable and sacrosanct. It was the politicians who provided the need to hold a ruler to account. If they were the true rulers, then it was they who should be responsible to their people. It was they who were expendable.

Ex-kings and claimants can do little but wait. They do so in the knowledge that it will take as great an upheaval to bring them back as it took to banish them. They are not without hope. In AD 33 the Republic of Rome gave way to an empire. In 1975 a king was returned to Spain. 'Whoever calls a political form an anachronism,' says Dr Habsburg, heir to the Austro-Hungarian throne, 'shows by this he has not learned from history.' This truism is about the only consolation to a monarch-in-waiting. However glamorous his title, he enjoys few advantages. 'Someone would have to tell me what these are because I certainly don't know,' King Rechad of Tunisia told me over a brown bread lobster sandwich in Fortnum and Mason. Besides working as a pin-striped businessman on the London oil markets, he was the Shadow of God on Earth, Sultan of Mascara, Sultan of Titteri, Sword and Glory of the Faith, Sultan of Sultans, Lord of Lords and 34th in line from the Prophet Mohammed. 'Perhaps if you 'phone up a restaurant, you get a table quicker than anyone else.'

PART ONE
CORONATION STREETS

1

Dear Old Twick

'Kings are justly called gods.'

JAMES I

'Royalty are people.'

ALEXANDER, GRAND DUKE OF RUSSIA

This century has seen the stocks of royalty reach an all-time low. The British monarchy, by contrast, has rarely been so popular. An estimated 650 million people watched Prince Charles's wedding, and hoped he would live happily ever after. Yet it is in England that this sad story of the death of kings must begin, with the judicial execution of another Charles.

Kings had been murdered and deposed before, but on that frosty day in January 1649 it was the principle of the monarch as a divine appointee – not his person – which was axed, and a precedent established that was to be repeated in the French Revolution, and the execution of Louis XVI, head of the oldest royal house in Europe. Thereafter the monarchy would be restored, but not its majesty. As Albert Camus wrote of Louis's condemnation, 'It symbolizes the secularization of our history and the dematerialization of the Christian God.'

Just as Charles's descendants found refuge in France after his death, that act of 1792 was to send every subsequent French monarch apart from Napoleon into English exile and divide the inheritance between three contesting families: the Bourbon brothers of Louis XVI, his Orléans cousins – known as 'the regicide dynasty' because one, Philippe 'Egalité', had voted for his death – and the heirs of Napoleon Bonaparte, who in 1804 had assumed the title of Emperor.

The Bourbons, who had entered England in dribs and drabs following the fall of the Bastille, were the first back on the throne. On Easter Day 1814, at 3 o'clock in the morning, a messenger scampered up the drive at Hartwell in Buckinghamshire. He was led by a candle down a long, dark corridor and admitted to the bedroom of a man who had for seven years tended his lilacs and laburnum and composed madrigals in the manner of Horace. The man, Louis XVIII, Louis XVI's younger brother, was woken and once on his gouty feet was informed that the Paris Senate had called for the return of their legitimate kings. He left Hartwell in a carriage drawn not by horses but by Englishmen. Insensitive, selfish and massively over-weight, he was known by them as 'Old Bungy Louis'. Shortly afterwards he sailed for Dover, aboard the *Royal Sovereignty*.

This was only the beginning of a regular British ferry service for foreign and deposed royalty.

The man who had flagged down William Pitt's carriage and asked the Prime Minister to allow Louis XVIII asylum in Buckinghamshire, was his tall, sensuous brother the Comte d'Artois. This distinguished adulterer had arrived in England in 1795 and finally taken digs in Baker Street, where in February 1800 he made his peace with his Orléans cousin, Louis Philippe, the son of Philippe 'Egalité'. With Napoleon's ascent not much was to be gained by prolonging a family feud. He played a nightly game of whist, and on the death of his ravishing mistress, surrendered himself to the service of God. On Louis XVIII's death in 1824 – he was so decayed that a valet found a loose toe when pulling off his socks – Artois acceded as Charles X. Neither as popular nor as shrewd as his brother (who had given France its first effective parliamentary régime), Charles was to be remembered more for having commissioned six Rossini operas than for his reign, which was characterized by a stubborn loyalty to his minority government. It ended with the July Revolution of 1830 after his dissolution of the new chamber and his imposition of a strict censorship on the press. He had found some difficulty in being a constitutional monarch. 'I would rather earn my bread,' he had boasted, 'than reign like the King of England.' Others reported him as saying he would rather hew wood.

Once off the throne, a lot of wood was hewn. Etiquette demanded that a king of France should eat squarely at a four-sided table, and during the flight from France the royal household could be seen at various inns sawing round tables to the correct shape. As with many monarchs, it was the trappings that replaced the power of the king. With a cargo that included two cows and five chamber pots, Charles X sailed from Cherbourg on the *Great Britain*. Installed at Holyrood Palace in Edinburgh, he resumed his games of whist. In between tricks, he squabbled for the rights of his legitimate successor – his grandson, the Comte de Chambord. In

1832 the climate became too much for him and he parted gracelessly, for Austria. Four years later he died of cholera.

Charles X's successor on the throne of France was his cousin, Louis Philippe, the Duke of Orléans. He was, as Victor Hugo observed, a rare man. Mirabeau had slapped him on the shoulder; Danton had said to him 'young man'. Yet he walked, unattended, through the Paris streets in a simple suit with a brolly under his arm.

In 1800, after three years spent in America, Louis Philippe had landed at Falmouth and settled in High Shot House, opposite the Crown Hotel, in Twickenham. For 132 years Twickenham was to provide a sanctuary for the Orléans and their descendants.

Though officially reconciled with the Bourbons, Louis Philippe remained unpopular with their entourage. On a visit to Louis XVIII at Hartwell he was spotted by Louis XVI's daughter whose legs promptly gave way in shock on meeting the son of the 'regicide' responsible for her father's death. While Louis XVIII had treated him with circumspection, Artois went out of his way to be affable. During Napoleon's brief return to France, which forced the King to flee from the Tuileries in his slippers, Louis Philippe was appointed Artois's ADC. When the Court fled to Ghent, he returned to Twickenham – this time to Orléans House – where he remained until 1817. He became a keen gardener, spading manure from Crown Lane on to his roses in what he whimsically called 'dear old Twick'. ('I bless heaven morning, noon and night that I'm in my peaceful house in old Twick on the banks of the Thames.') He also became a friend of Turner and Wellington – and an Anglophile. 'The safety of Europe, that of the world, and the future happiness and independence of mankind, rests upon the preservation and independence of England.' Though proud of being a French Prince, he admitted also to being an Englishman, 'in terms of my principles, my opinions and all my habits'. These habits stuck long after his Bourbon cousins welcomed him back to France in 1817. When, having succeeded them, he was visited by Disraeli at the Tuileries, he insisted on carving the ham. It was a trick, he boasted, that he had learned from a waiter in a Bucklersbury eating-house.

As King, Louis Philippe was to survive the many assassination attempts which punctuated his reign and gave rise to the saying, 'For shooting kings there is no close season'. He was unable, however, to stop the tide of revolution in 1848. In February of that year, disguised unimaginatively in thick goggles and a greatcoat as William Smith, he was accompanied by his 'nephew', the British Vice-Consul, aboard the channel packet *Express*. It was a close shave. He talked too loud but the ship had sailed by the time the gendarmes arrived to arrest him.

Things were not the same in dear old Twick. The manure on which he had nourished his roses had found its way into his drinking water. While the drains were cleaned he renewed his acquaintance with pubs by taking rooms in the Star and Garter. On one occasion during his stay, while wandering on foot through the town, he was accosted by a retired innkeeper.

'Surely you remember me, Your Majesty,' the man said, pumping his hands. 'I kept The Crown.'

Only a foreigner could have been so British in his reply.

'That's more than I did.'

Louis Philippe died in August 1850, his face crumpled with pleurisy. 'Not long ago,' wrote Charles Greville from a room in Brighton, 'his life was the most important in the world and his death would have produced a profound sensation and general consternation. Now hardly more importance attaches to the event than there would be to the death of one of the old bathing women opposite my window.'

The last sovereign of France, in a century of divided royalties, was Louis Napoleon. One day before Waterloo, at the age of seven, he had been lifted by his uncle, the dynamic Corsican, to see the troops parading in the Place du Carrousel. He never forgot the experience. 'I believe that from time to time men are created whom I may call men of destiny,' he later wrote. 'In their hands the fate of the country is bound up. I believe that I myself am one of these men.' Banished from France by both the Bourbons and Orléans, he spent his childhood in Switzerland before sailing to England where he hoped to obtain more publicity for himself and his cause. In May 1831 Louis Napoleon stepped off the *Royal George* at Dover, a taciturn, overdressed man with short legs, a large head and a passion for singers and actresses whom he was to drive about London in a carriage painted with eagles. What energies he had left were channelled into restoring the Bonaparte dynasty. He scribbled a few strident pamphlets, giving the impression that on the subject of politics he was 'as mad as a hatter'. Then he translated these ideas into action, and confirmed it.

One October day in 1836 Louis Philippe sat with his cabinet in the Tuileries. An urgent telegraph from Strasbourg had been cut off by the fog, but it spoke of an insurrection led by Louis Napoleon and a Colonel of

Artillery. There was little cause for concern. Three hours after he had introduced himself to the 4th Artillery and inspired shouts of 'Long live the Emperor!' Louis Napoleon was denounced as an impostor. Undeterred, he made his way back to Carlton House, and planned another coup.

In the summer of 1840, the year that Napoleon's remains were returned to Europe, he chartered the steamer *Edinburgh Castle* for a pleasure cruise and filled it with horses, uniforms and guns bought in Birmingham. The departure from Gravesend was delayed because one of the crew insisted on rowing back to get some cigars. Eventually anchor was weighed and the ship slipped into the Channel. Two days later Louis Napoleon found himself in a Boulogne prison.

He spent six years in the fortress of Ham on the Somme marshes, writing more pamphlets – this time on sugar-beet and pauperism. Only the government of Nicaragua applied for his release. One day, taking matters into his own hands, he shaved his beard and whiskers, donned a black wig and put on workman's trousers. Wearing four-inch wooden clogs to make him taller, he lifted a plank on to his shoulder and made for the gate. As he approached the sentry, the white clay pipe drooping from his mouth fell to the ground. He picked up the pieces, continued on and arrived in London on Derby day.

The Chartist risings of 1848 were the nearest England came to revolution. In April of that year Louis Napoleon performed one of his last public duties before becoming President of the Second French Republic, and soon afterwards Emperor Napoleon III of France. Enrolling as a Special Constable, he was sworn in at Marlborough Street Magistrates Court and despatched with three other gentlemen to Trafalgar Square. His only slice of the action was to arrest a drunken old woman. Five months later he quitted his house in King Street for Paris, leaving an unmade bed and a bath full of water.

Twenty-three years later busts of him were being thrown into the Seine from the Pont Neuf. The Prussians had laid siege to Paris and he was in prison again. 'When I am free,' he wrote to his wife, 'it is in England that I wish to live with you . . . in a little cottage with bow windows and creepers.' In 1871 he joined her at Camden Place, Chislehurst, an austere red-brick house with very hot rooms.

Though he had grown fat and grey, and his moustaches were unwaxed and uncurled, Louis Napoleon remained a figure of romance for women.

One wanted to have a son by him, believing it would be the Saviour of France. For men, and religious fanatics in particular, he continued to be the Antichrist prophesied in the Book of Daniel. These images belied the old man who pottered about on the common in Kent with pennies in his pockets for children and oddball praise for the cricketers. (After one spectacular catch he sent a message to long-on asking him to do it again.) Even his final pamphlet, *Les Forces Militaires de la France en 1870*, lacked the vigour once addressed to the sugar-beet question. 'When one has fallen from so high,' he told the press some months before his death in 1873, 'one's first feeling is not the desire to mount the pinnacle once again, but to seek the causes of one's defeat in order to explain one's conduct and combat calumny, while recognizing one's faults.'

When Louis Napoleon fell the Orléans sons and grandchildren of Louis Philippe left their homes in Twickenham for France. Their prayers had been answered. 'It is our country we ask for, our country that we love, that our family has always served loyally,' they had written in a petition to the Corps Legislatif. 'Truly for the exile nothing can take the place of the lost fatherland.' At the Lord Warden Hotel in Dover some members of the family came face to face with the returning Emperor. There was an embarrassing pause. The Empress broke it with a curtsy and passed on in silence.

With the collapse of the Second Empire in 1870, most prospects of a return to monarchy in France came to an end. To make such a restoration likely, should the opportunity arise, Louis Philippe's grandson, the Count of Paris, decided to unite the rival royalist factions; he did so by recognizing his Bourbon cousin, the Comte de Chambord and senior representative of the family, as sole claimant.

Grandson of Charles X, and revered by his supporters as Henry V, the lame and stocky Comte de Chambord took the cue. In the summer of 1870 he left his Austrian castle for the French border. 'I am under no illusion,' he wrote in a note to his wife. 'I know that where I am going I will probably meet my death.' He survived, probably because he never crossed the border, but a manifesto he delivered promising a truly national government with 'right as its base, honesty as its means and moral grandeur as its goal' was completely ignored. Chambord's behaviour proved to be as empty-headed as his prose. On two occasions, in 1871 and 1873, there was a majority of monarchists in the Assembly and restoration was there for the taking. Chambord queered his pitch by refusing to acknowledge the tricolour. Instead, he insisted on the Bourbon banner, the fleur–de–lys. 'In the glorious folds of this spotless standard, I will bring you order and liberty, FRENCHMEN! Henry V cannot abandon the white flag of Henry IV.' And so it was he who was abandoned, the first man 'to give up the throne for a napkin'. According to one historian, 'the failure of the Third Restoration announced the doom of all hereditary monarchies of the crowned and anointed sort, not only in Europe but throughout the entire world.'

Chambord died childless in 1883, his claim passing back to the Orléans and the Count of Paris, who was styled Philippe VII. By now, however, the Republic had consolidated itself. In 1886, at a grand reception in Paris, the Count of Paris's daughter, Amélie, married Don Carlos, heir to the Portuguese throne. The four thousand dignitaries who attended were seen by *Figaro* as the personnel of a future monarchy. The republicans saw them as an open challenge. In the following month a law of exile was rushed through the Assembly. 'The territory of the French Republic,' it stated, 'is and remains forbidden to the heads of former ruling families and their direct heirs.' They were given three days to pack. As one observer commented, watching a retainer bid farewell to the Count, 'Can you imagine a greater torture than receiving condolences at one's own death and assisting at one's own funeral.'

And so, sixteen years after they had left, the Orléans returned to Twickenham.

One week after Prince William of England was born, I drove along the Great Western Road to Syon House. Originally a Brigittine monastery named after the City of our God, Syon is now owned by the descendants of William I, the Lion King of Scotland. It is a potent reminder of the forces which have prevented God from having a representative in the political system.

Most of the blinds were down in the Long Gallery, where I met the present Duke of Northumberland. In the shadows where Thomas More had tested the divinity of the Holy Maid of Kent and Lady Jane Grey had fainted on being told she was Queen of England, we talked of insect repellents.

Long before Adam got his hands on the narrow gallery, making it appear wider than it was, Cromwell had paced there planning the second phase of the Civil War. In 1647, after seven peers and fifty-eight commoners had resolved 'to live and die with the army', he marched through London and seized Westminster and the Tower. When, two years later, Charles I was beheaded as a tyrant, traitor and public enemy, it was over a decade before people could shout 'Long live the King!'

There is no ha-ha at Syon, just the Thames which makes a swan's-neck curve for a few miles until it reaches Twickenham, until 1431 the original site of the house. Today there are no remains of this site and few signs of the more recent Orléans influx. Most of their houses – High Shot, Mount Lebanon, Bute House – have been demolished. What remains of Orléans House has been turned into an art gallery. In 1964 the red-brick, white-shuttered York House, home of the Count of Paris, was sold to the Twickenham County Council. If one peers into the backs of the fireplaces one may still make out the odd fleurs-de-ly. The Crown, a pink building on the Richmond Road, is also in new hands, and gives no hint of former clients, nor had anyone heard of them.

The Count of Paris, a man who might have made history, settled down at York House to write it instead. While his wife, a masculine woman who smoked a pipe, spent her days in the hunting field, he devoted himself to an account of the American Civil War and the British Trades Union movement. He died in 1894 and was buried, with eighty-two other members of his family, inside the Orléans vault in the chapel of St Charles Borromeo, Weybridge. His body was not to be taken back to France until the heir to the throne could pray on his tomb.

His own son and heir, the Duke of Orléans, became the uncrowned Philippe VIII – and President of the Twickenham Rowing Club. Born in York House and a product of Sandhurst, he was very much at home in London, despite its thick fogs and thin coffee. Whenever he had to address a gathering of French royalists he would sigh and mutter under his breath, 'What asses . . . ' This may have been due to an unhappy experience as a young man. He had been filled with a desire to serve out his military service in France and in 1890, wearing a false beard, he reached Paris, where he was promptly put in prison for having disobeyed the law of exile. Twenty years later, in the autumn of 1910, he was on the quayside at Plymouth to receive his sister, Amélie, now the Queen Mother of Portugal, whose marriage had prompted this law. She was returning to the place of her birth on board the royal yacht *Victoria and Albert*. With her in exile she brought her eighteen-year-old son King Manoel of Portugal, the great-great-grandson of Louis Philippe.

Two and a half years earlier, on 1 February 1908, King Carlos, Queen Amélie and their two sons, the Crown Prince and Dom Manoel, had landed from the ferry boat at the Praca do Commercio in Lisbon. As they climbed into an open carriage, the Queen was presented with a bouquet of flowers. Suddenly a bearded man jumped on to the rear of the vehicle. He was a well-mannered ex-cavalry sergeant and schoolteacher who had given lessons to the children of various ladies-in-waiting. He was called Buica and he carried a gun won as a prize in a shooting match and presented to him by the King. He lowered it into the carriage and fired twice. One bullet hit King Carlos in the neck, passing through the carotid artery. The other struck the Crown Prince in the face. The Queen was hitting Buica with her flowers when an officer sent a sword through his back. More shots rang out from the pillars of the Ministry of the Interior, one slightly wounding Dom Manoel's arm. The coachman drove on. In the stunned streets a young girl suddenly went mad. She howled like a dog until nightfall.

Not for the first time, or the last, was England indirectly responsible for breaking up a throne. At the start of his reign King Carlos had received a humiliating ultimatum from Lord Salisbury, following a dispute between the two countries over parts of Mashonaland in Africa. In Lisbon crowds smashed the windows of pro-British newspapers, but the insouciant King gave way. He was promptly accused of having insulted the flag.

The republicans fed and grew on his unpopularity. Loyalty to the inadequate, selfish Braganças further decayed when Carlos accepted the order of the Garter after the issue was settled.

There was little sorrow or regret at Carlos's death, and less expectation that his young son Manoel could achieve anything important. 'I am without knowledge and experience,' he admitted. It did not help that he was also ill-advised both by his government (five cabinets fell in two years), and by his mother, Queen Amélie.

A tall, ambitious, tough woman who had once rescued a fisherman from drowning, she was looked on as the man of the family. She combined a belief that 'a Princess of France must never give way' with a compulsive desire to do good. While she inspected her charities, buying fuel-saving stores for vagrants and feeding shipwrecked sailors, Manoel generously promised to appropriate no money that parliament did not vote him. While she underlined the necessity for Manoel 'to make himself the initiator and leader of the vast reforms needed for the safety of

9

Portugal', he took himself off to Paris and fell in with a kittenish dancing-girl called Gaby Deslys. His friendship with the French girl and the garters he strapped round her legs may have launched Deslys's career, but it finished his own.

His country was bankrupt: it was a time which called for economies in the royal household, not a lavish display of favours. His reception of Deslys at the palace of Necessidades was followed by news that the Queen Mother, his grandmother Maria Pia, had paid neither her gas bills, which amounted to some £12,000, nor a Parisian jeweller to whom she owed 26,000 francs for a necklace. The anti-monarchist cabals had a field day. Members of secret societies such as the Woodcutters, who dressed up in monks' cowls, went wild. Ten days after Manoel made a speech from the throne appealing for loyalty and promising everything that people could desire, Portugal revolted.

Manoel had laughed when Foxy Ferdinand, Tsar of Bulgaria, fell off his horse. 'Laugh away, my dear cousin, but my seat in the saddle is safer than yours on the throne,' Ferdinand had cuttingly replied. He was right, and it needed only a spark to prove it. On the evening of 3 October 1910 Dr Miguel Bombarda, a prominent republican and the superintendent of the Lisbon lunatic asylum, was greeted by a former inmate, Rebello dos Santos. Dos Santos had been discharged from the asylum against the wishes of Bombarda, who diagnosed him as incurable.

'Well, Rebello, what brings you here today?' Bombarda asked his former patient, who answered by producing a revolver and shooting him dead. Laying the blame at the door of pro-government 'reactionaries', the republicans used this event as a pretext for a rising that had already been planned.

Manoel was entertaining the President of Brazil at a residence in Belem. When he heard about the shooting he returned to the palace of Necessidades. At 2 o'clock in the morning he heard shots fired by the gunners of the 1st Battery of Artillery. They were joined by the men of the 16th Regiment of Infantry. Manoel spent a frantic night telephoning for help. The news was not encouraging. The coup was being led by a colonel from the north who earlier had requested a transfer to the capital, warning him of possible trouble. Even Manoel's servants were manoeuvring to overthrow him. At daybreak he took heart at the sight of two of his ships in the Tagus. Then he noticed the red and green colours of the republicans flying

from the halyards, and the cruisers *Adamastor* and *Sao Rafael* opened fire.
The first shell damaged a chimney. Another went off in the next room.
Shelled out of his palace by his own navy, Manoel escaped by the garden
gate and joined his mother in Mafra. Before leaving with her for the
coastal town of Ericeira, he embraced the commandant of the Military
College. As soon as he was out of sight, this man too gave orders to hoist
the red and green flag.

On 5 October 1910 the last King of Portugal and of the Algarves, on this
side and also on the other side of the sea in Africa, Lord of the Conquest,
navigation and trade of Guinea, Ethiopia, Persia and India, was rowed out
to the royal yacht *Amelia* with his mother. 'The King cannot run away,'
she raged, speaking, as usual, for him. 'He much prefers to die.' Yet the
small fishing boat that returned to the shore bore only a farewell letter.

Constrained by circumstances over which I have no control, I find
myself obliged to embark on the yacht *Amelia*. I am Portuguese and I
shall always be so. It is my conviction that I have always and in all
circumstances done my duty as a king and placed my person and my life
at the service of my country. I hope the country persuaded of my
affection and my devotion, will recognize the fact. Long live Portugal.
Manoel. Pray give this letter all possible publicity.

The statement with its heartfelt PS had no effect, for a republic had been
proclaimed, and the first law drafted. 'The dynasty of Bragança who have
deliberately destroyed the peace in the country is banished from Portugal
for ever.'

Manoel landed at Gibraltar dressed in the clothes in which he had left,
the dust of Ericeira still on his hat. He had had to borrow a dinner jacket
from the Governor's ADC. In some embarrassment, George V despatched the royal yacht *Victoria and Albert* to collect the couple. When it
finally steamed into Plymouth Sound, where Manoel had one year earlier
been saluted by the British fleet, the Duke of Orléans, Amélie's brother
and the French Pretender, was there to greet them. A wheel had come full
circle.

Mother and son rented Abercorn House in King's Road, Richmond –
York House, Amélie's birthplace, having been sold five years before. 'I
shall stand my ground,' she crowed (without having much choice), con-

11

vinced that the condition of mankind was bound up with monarchy. 'I am in a state of inward certainty, I might say of revelation as to its truth.' Happy in this knowledge, she moved first to Germany, then to France where she died in 1951.

Manoel spent the first months in exile unfolding the papers from Lisbon and reading how more of his dearest confidants were saluting the new flag. So that he could travel abroad, an English diplomat drew up a hand-written passport requesting foreign customs authorities to let him pass freely. In 1913, having given up hopes of his dancer, he married Princess Augusta of Hohenzollern. The same year they moved into Fulwell Park House, Twickenham, where they spent the rest of their childless marriage.

Augusta's natural lights burnt very dim, apparently; the only thing to glare, especially during the war, was her German origin. One day, after she had visited the gunpowder mills at the bottom of her garden, there was an explosion which killed two men. Rumour had it that Augusta was responsible.

Manoel was only twenty-one when he left Portugal. Whereas many authors consider a king to be a fit subject, Manoel spent the rest of his life studying authors, in particular those of sixteenth-century Portuguese works. In his catalogue to early Portuguese books in his collection, he hinted at the reason for this escape. 'To recognize what the love of one's country can be,' he wrote, 'it is necessary to live far away from it and deprived of its atmosphere.'

Without his mother to spur him on, he was not a man to sigh much for his throne, though now and again he was proclaimed King in places like Chaves and Oporto. He lived instead the life of a squire, fishing for perch in the river Crane and growing roses like his ancestors before him. And like them he was hugged to the suburban bosom of Twickenham; known as 'His Majesty', he was made President of the Piscatorial Society, and occasionally presented with a cup in the Gardening Association's annual competition. He reciprocated by holding garden parties, raising funds for the Church Hall and sending donations to the local Pansy Day collection.

Music was another pastime. In his youth he had wanted to conduct an orchestra; in exile he had to content himself with playing the organ. Prince Christopher of Greece, who claimed to have been offered the throne of Portugal in 1912 – an offer he refused – was affected by his playing. He became a close friend of Manoel after meeting him in the Pump Room at Harrogate and judged him to be 'one of the best amateur pianists I have ever heard'. He was also taken by Manoel's sense of humour, following a visit which began with polite conversation at the table and ended under it with the squirting of soda siphons – an episode which may tell one more about Prince Christopher than Manoel.

During the First World War Manoel devoted himself to hospital duties and made repeated visits and endowments to orthopaedic centres all over the country. His involvement did not end with the war. I watched one rare piece of newsreel, a few feet of nitrate film dug up from the vaults in Elstree, which shows him opening a new ward for babies in Shrewsbury's Orthopaedic Hospital. Dressed in a fur collar and hat, leaning heavily on his stick, he snips the ribbon. Outside the nurses cheer, their skirts ballooning in the wind: they look rather like chorus girls. The year was 1926, and his Queen had often been seen in tears. I wondered if he was thinking of Gaby Deslys. Then the film snapped.

Manoel liked the cinema. He sat in Richmond's picture palaces, wrapped in a thick coat and smoothing his moustache. Perhaps it was another form of escape, like his passion for tennis. Bunny Ryan used to play with him at Queen's. 'He had an extremely good forehand which I used to play to because it made the game better for me. His backhand was weak.' So too was his health. On Friday 1 July 1932 he had been watching Wimbledon, as he had done every year. The next day, complaining of a sore throat, he visited a specialist and was sent to bed. Half an hour later he had a coughing attack. By two in the afternoon he was dead. He was forty-two.

After lying in the Orléans vault at St Charles Borromeo, Weybridge, Manoel's coffin was taken by HMS *Concord* to Lisbon and placed in the Bragança mausoleum in the church of Sao Vicente. Manoel's widow returned to Germany, where she remarried. Nothing remains of Fulwell Park House. The white lodge was pulled down in 1934 to make way for a housing estate, and its marble mantels, five capital boilers and six expensive porcelain baths were put up for sale. Occasionally a slab of coloured quartz is still unearthed, but the only relics from the house are to be found in St James's Church, Pope's Grove. Near a memorial window, stained with the Bragança crest, are Manoel's sanctuary lamp, his communion plate, and his organ.

As for the winter garden, the peacocks and their owners, they are now commemorated in place-names such as Orléans Garage, where Manoel had his Rolls-Royce serviced, and street signs like Manoel Road, Augusta

Road, Lisbon Avenue and Portugal Gardens. The family is not wholly forgotten, though. One day in the grounds of the Fulwell estate, now a public park, I met an old man who remembered Manoel. 'He wasn't ill, you know. He committed suicide. But it wasn't done for people in his position to do that, so things were hushed up.' How did he know? He had a friend then who was an ambulance driver. This man was called to the house that afternoon in 1932 and overheard the cause of Manoel's death.

Such rumours are not to be taken seriously. A different account was given to me by an amateur medium who was living, ex-directory, in a council house on the spot of Fulwell Park House. One day the King climbed out of an apple tree in her garden. After several more ghost appearances he told her who he was. He was in a state of understandable distress, having, he explained, been murdered by his wife. The medium was sympathetic. On the fiftieth anniversary of Manoel's death she had organized masses to be said for him throughout Twickenham.

2

'Gone with the Windsors'

' . . . the monarchical institution has now outlived its usefulness.'
JAMES MAXTON MP ON ABDICATION OF EDWARD VIII

The best view of Lisbon is from the opposite bank of the Tagus, beneath the arms of an enormous statue of Christ. One hand points across the river – known because of the sun's reflection as the River of Straw – to the far east of the city, and the white dome of Sao Vicente, where King Manoel is buried; the other towards the red palace of Necessidades, from where he fled. The majestic suspension bridge, one of the longest in Europe, begins its curve above the water just to the west of Necessidades. Today it is known as Ponte 25 Abril, in honour of the bloodless revolution of 1974. Originally it was named after Dr Salazar, the dictator responsible for making Portugal a haven for Europe's ex-royalty. The rechristening is ironic since it was usually a revolution which had brought them here.

From 1932 until his retirement after a stroke in 1968, Salazar ran his country like a book-keeper. The son of a bailiff, he was a devout, romantic man with a scholarly stoop, and 'shy as a badger'. Summoned to office from his Chair of Political Economy in Coimbra University, he continued to lead a life of austerity. In his official residence he lived on £30 a week, looked after by an old housekeeper. He kept chickens and rabbits in the courtyard and wrapped a rug around his knees when he worked. 'Everything Salazar stands for is the antithesis of Bolshevism,' wrote one contemporary. 'To mention Bolshevism to a Salazar man is like dropping vinegar on a freshly opened oyster.' Perhaps it was for this reason, as well as the realization that they would bring in money, that he allowed the most

15

famous refugees from Communism to set up a royal colony near Lisbon. At the end of the First World War Portugal had been one of the few countries in Europe to accept the last Emperor of Austria-Hungary. At the end of the Second World War it was almost the only country which agreed to receive the royal families of Romania, Spain, Italy, France and Bulgaria. They came because it was quiet and cheap, and in the knowledge that if the political situation in Europe got further out of hand they could leave easily for America.

To Christ's left, through the 25 April Bridge, where the River of Straw becomes the Atlantic, can be seen the twin resorts of Cascais and Estoril where they settled; and behind, in the mist, the hills of Sintra where the last claimant to arrive has made his home. He is the young Duke of Bragança, heir to King Manoel's throne.

Though Portugal's last king had died in England, it was to be a former British monarch who set the fashion for his royal cousins to while away their days near Lisbon. The late journalist and author Hester Marsden-Smedley remembered both men. On her first day at school, the head-mistress of West Heath told her there were two things she could not do. One was to laugh at the jittery Lord Dysart in church. The other was to continue the crocodile across Richmond Common when King Manoel was seen walking there. Usually the orders came from the back, but on such an occasion the head of the crocodile snapped an order to turn in the opposite direction. 'I always longed to be head, because I wouldn't have said a thing.'

In the summer of 1940 she was working for the *Sunday Express* in Lisbon, the only foreign woman journalist there. She arrived without a visa and the British consul, a man named King, was telephoned by the authorities.

'What shall we do? We have this woman who hasn't got a visa.'

'Put her in prison,' replied King, with the usual reaction of a diplomat to a distressed British subject.

On her release she attended a party given by the Ambassador, Sir Walter Selby, for the Duke and Duchess of Windsor.

'I walked along and curtsied to the Duke, and then I came to the Duchess and did the same. If my curtsy should mean anything to anyone, she should have it – and she did. She was older than me and the wife of the former King of England.'

Next day Marcus Cheke, the Press Attaché, telephoned her.

16

'Someone told me you curtsied to the Duchess. Is this true?'

When she informed him that it was, he threatened to have her returned to England. One thing the British government would not do – the one thing the Duke of Windsor wished of them – was to accord the former Bessie Wallis Warfield of Maryland the honours due to royalty. This impasse was one of the reasons the couple had arrived in Lisbon. It was also the reason they stayed so long.

Although he did not see it as such, Portugal was a natural place for the Duke of Windsor to bide his time. To begin with, the two countries were linked by the world's oldest alliance, the Treaty of Windsor, which had been signed in 1386 and had placed an English queen upon the throne. Two and a half centuries after some tipsy crusaders from Suffolk had helped free Lisbon from the Moors, John of Gaunt's daughter, Philippa of Lancaster, married John I of Portugal in Oporto.

This ice-queen, who had been taught the astrolabes by Chaucer, soon returned sobriety to the Court. She made an English parson her Chancellor and stopped her husband pecking his ladies-in-waiting on the lips. More important, she gave Portugal a son whose expeditions were to change the country from a far-flung kingdom on the edge of Europe to the world's leading empire.

Henry the Navigator, who was born in the Rua dos Inglezes, Oporto, and christened after his uncle Henry Bolingbroke, himself sat nobly at Cape St Vincent and never went further than Tangiers. But from his windswept fort of Sagres he sent out ship after ship to the African coast.

'Go back and learn some more,' he told his returning captains. 'Go further.'

And after he died, they did. Only one man had passed the Cape of Good Hope before the Portuguese – according to contemporary pulpit-bashers – and that was Jonah in the whale's belly. But for Henry, one Frederick Sudley's great-grandson, Vasco de Gama, would never have discovered India, nor would Brazil have been claimed for Portugal; and Rodrigo de Triana would not have scampered down from the crow's nest to tell Columbus he had spotted the New World.

The fruits of Henry's work were reaped by Manoel I, known as Manoel the Fortunate – a luckier man than his descendant and a king who gave his name to Portugal's only style of architecture – the Manueline. The style is infectious. One writer talks of 'sucking fabulous wealth from the abundant breasts of old Asia', and it is this wealth, acquired by exchanging Bibles for baubles, the Gospel for gold, which is reflected in the extravagant motifs which disgrace the inhabitable follies of Sintra; pillars that look like trees, engraved with ropes and anchors; cables and corals, spices and ivory.

The Treaty of Windsor survived unbroken, even during the English Civil War, when Charles I's dashing nephew, Prince Rupert, received both sympathy and sanctuary in the Tagus. In fact on Charles's death, only the King of Portugal extended the traditional message of goodwill to the new sovereign. Because of the alliance, Catherine of Bragança came to London and married Charles II, bestowing, with her dowry of Bombay and Tangiers, an itch for empire. And also because of the alliance, the British transported Lisbon's Court to Rio when Napoleon invaded, and then set Wellington loose upon the French. Wellington's only black mark was the Convention of Sintra, which allowed the defeated French commander, Junot, a safe passage for his men and his booty. Seteais is the beautiful palace in Sintra where the signing is supposed to have taken place. It is so called because on hearing these terms the Portuguese sighed seven times.

The saw-toothed hills of Sintra, Byron's 'glorious Eden', lie fifteen miles from Lisbon. Some quirk of nature whips the damp Atlantic spray over this westernmost tip of the Continent. Anything grows in the tropical mist, which makes the landscape with its cliffs and cataracts as gothic as the palaces that crest these hills – and the people who live within. Sintra has been a mecca for the English, and for royalty, ever since Philippa settled her Court there in the summer months. To Sintra came the literati. Southey wrote 'Thalaba' and his lost *History of Portugal* beneath the Moorish battlements. The outrageous author William Beckford settled first at Ramalhao and then at the Moorish *quinta* of Montserrate. In its gardens he found a substitute for his social ambitions, becoming 'too much engaged in the royalties of nature to think of inferior royalties'. Byron wrote part of 'Childe Harold' in an inn run by a Welsh lady, Mrs Lawrence. Wilfred Blunt stayed at the same inn. The Earl of Lytton left his manuscript of 'Seraphim' in her loo where it was used by a maid to wipe her bottom. Perhaps the most immortal lines were inscribed on the same lavatory wall by a respectable English lady: 'I came to this place twice, for it is very nice.'

Many others came to the area. Only one, Henry Fielding stayed. He

18

died in Lisbon. No one knows exactly where he is buried in the English cemetery; his tomb may cover the bones of an idiot. He died one year before the earthquake on All Souls' Day, 1755. When the dust had settled and the fires blown out it had destroyed 300 palaces, 110 churches and 10 monasteries; and it had convinced Voltaire that there could be no God. One of the buildings demolished was the English nunnery where the nuns of Syon had finally settled in 1594, after the Convent had been dissolved by Elizabeth. In 1802 Earl Percy, the third Duke of Northumberland, visited them with a silver model of Syon. The abbess remarked dryly that though he had the house they still had the keys.

'Very true,' he replied. 'But I have taken the precaution of altering all the locks since then.'

It was his father, the second Duke of Northumberland, who had presented a copy of the entrance gates of Syon to John VI of Portugal. He took them with him on his exile to Brazil and had them erected at his country residence three miles from Rio. They now form the entrance to the town zoo.

The most celebrated visitor to Portugal before the Duke of Windsor was his grandfather, Edward VII. For his visit as Prince of Wales in 1876, English carpenters had come to build pavilions, an English musician had arrived to teach the local bands to play the anthem, and it was even said by one journalist that strenuous efforts had been made to create an English fog. All that Edward took out of Portugal was a Sintra donkey, which he sent home to Sandringham, and two shirts. Perhaps in protest, one of the horses drawing the royal carriage stopped dead, and despite bayonet and umbrella prods, could not be persuaded to move.

In 1903 Edward returned as King. He stayed with his cousin and friend King Carlos in Necessidades, he adjudicated at pigeon-shoots, and he opened a park in his name, Parque Eduardo Setimo. It was not enough. Memories of the English ultimatum were still fresh; yet again the royal landau was to stay put when one of the horses registered another equine protest and refused to budge.

Edward sailed away on the *Victoria and Albert*, the yacht that was to take Manoel to England in 1910, one year after he had once more ratified the Treaty of Windsor.

On 25 April 1931 the SS *Arlanza* arrived in Lisbon from Pernambuco. It was carrying Edward, Prince of Wales, back from another royal tour. The journey to South America had yet again confirmed his restless spirit. 'It never left him,' said Hector Bolitho, one of the bow-tied commentators of the age. 'And it wasn't his fault. It was greatly our own, and it led to the abdication.'

After inspecting a regiment of Portuguese troops the Prince of Wales proceeded to Estoril, a resort ten miles along the coast. Exchanging his uniform for a pair of white trousers and a black beret, he spent the afternoon swinging his clubs on the golf course. Before he left he signed the visitors' book. That winter, during a cold foggy week-end at Melton Mowbray, he first set eyes on Mrs Simpson.

It was nine years before he returned to Portugal. A lot had changed. The Germans had invaded Paris. London was about to be blitzed into rubble. And to catch the woman he loved, the man who had dispersed the shadow of war with his smile had given up the glory she now wanted. Invested with a great deal more of human nature than divinity, Edward VIII had renounced his throne. 'Make no mistake,' Winston Churchill told Lady Airlie, 'he can't live without her.'

On the night of his final broadcast – from Augusta Tower in Windsor Castle – while people drummed placards announcing 'Abdication means revolution', he drove to Portsmouth. The Admiralty yacht *Enchantress* had been replaced at the last moment by a ship with a less apt name, the destroyer *Fury*.

It was after four in the morning when the *Fury* slipped anchor for Boulogne, taking the champion of the unemployed to join them, with clothes to last a week and a few photographs.

A marked change came over the Duke of Windsor in his self-imposed exile. The man who had been King began to quarrel over crumbs. He had paid the bill for preferring a private to a public life, but service was not included. In France he argued over tips in restaurants. He upset the army by getting his chef demobilized and restored to his kitchen. More seriously, he listened to his goading wife.

Hitler had said of her, 'She would have made a good Queen.' Plainly she agreed, and if she was not going to get that chance at least she would have the honours due to her by this third marriage. It was not enough merely to be voted one of the world's best-dressed women.

Shortly before the wedding ceremony at the Château de Candé in the

Loire, news came from England that Mrs Simpson was not to be accorded with the same rank as her sisters-in-law. She was to be Duchess of Windsor still.

The Duke's desire for a useful position in which to serve his country coupled with his obsession for her status, became the guiding lights by which he steered. He made their staff stand in her presence and at all times address her as Your Royal Highness. Then he tried to make Churchill and his government do the same.

It seemed a squalid irrelevance at a time when King and cabinet had war on their hands. The Duke agreed. 'From a distance, what I insisted on may look to be of small value. But the perspective of my life had changed and the matter loomed mightily large for me.' In May 1940, when the Germans invaded France, he ordered his friend, Fruity Metcalfe, to take his cairn terriers to join the Duchess. Then, deserting Metcalfe and his post as liaison officer between the French and British armies, he followed the dogs. The couple fled across the Spanish border in a convoy consisting of the Duke's Buick, a Citroën and a lorry for their luggage.

In Madrid a telegram from Churchill awaited them. 'Come back to England immediately,' he urged, frantic to have them whisked off the Continent and out of the enemy's clutches. 'Two flying boats will be at Lisbon to pick you up and your party.' In the urgency of Churchill's demand, the Duke saw a means of bartering for the two things he wanted: an important job for himself and three initials for his wife.

Neil Hogg, Lord Hailsham's brother, was Second Secretary at the Embassy in Lisbon. On 2 July 1940 he met the Windsors at the Elvas–Badajoz border. After waiting for the Duke to wash his dogs in a stream, he accompanied the convoy to a house near Lisbon belonging to the banker Ricardo Espirito Santo.

The bank of Espirito Santo e Commercial has been nationalized but it still bears the family name. Holy Ghost and Commerce: profitable merger of mind and body.

Ricardo's granddaughter, Mary, lives today in the large pink house in Cascais on a stretch of coastline known as the Boca do Inferno – the Mouth of Hell. She spends her time restoring ceramics and looking after the Espirito Santo Museum in Lisbon. Ever since *Now* magazine published an article claiming that her family had been pro-Nazi she has not liked journalists. It was consequently difficult to see her. When I eventually gained access to the house, I found a thin, dark woman with a sad face that dissolved into frequent smiles. After leading me outside to the deserted swimming-pool, we walked back on to the terrace.

'The sea-spray is very bad for the house. Look,' she said, rubbing one of the pillars and holding out her hand, 'it just crumbles.'

We came inside and sat at the end of a table in the blue-tiled dining-room.

'I don't know anything about his stay here, just that my grandfather was a friend of his and his brother, the Duke of Kent. I know one story about the Duke of Kent. My grandfather gave him a large urn when he stayed here. Some years later in London, he saw it in a window for sale.' She smiled. 'I think that's funny.'

Before I left she went upstairs and came down with some photographs. 'I don't know if you're interested in these,' she said guardedly. They showed the Duchess by the pool in sunglasses, the Duke playing golf, and the pair of them standing by the crumbling pillars. In all the photographs their faces were tense.

A lot of nonsense has been written about the Duke's four weeks in Lisbon. Thriller writers have made mischief of a Nazi plot to abduct him and his wife and return them to the throne. Even a recent study of the Duke's war has glossed over questions which may never be answered.

To deal first with what is certain.

On the night of 3 July the British Ambassador, Sir Walford Selby – a man described by Hester Marsden-Smedley as 'very nice and very dim' – arrived at the house with another telegram from Churchill.

'You threatened me with what amounted to arrest,' the Duke of Windsor later wrote to him. Technically he was still a serving British officer, as the Prime Minister made clear. 'Your Royal Highness has taken active military rank and refusal to obey direct orders of competent military authority would create a serious situation. I hope it will not be necessary for such orders to be sent.'

Selby, it seemed, had retained his passport, and it may have been due to this combined pressure that the Duke agreed on a return to London without either of his conditions being met.

Then another telegram arrived, offering him the post of Governor and Commander-in-Chief of the Bahamas.

'It's not an appointment,' the Duchess complained, with her facility for one-liners; 'it's a more of a disappointment.' The Duke accepted, but he too thought it wretched. When someone congratulated him on the task of looking after so many islands, he turned on him bitterly. 'Name one,' he said.

There followed a month's delay before the couple sailed. The reason for this remains mysterious. It is hard to believe that the government, so eager to have them removed from the scene, should have left them to make their own getaway when Hitler's troops were on the Pyrenees. It is also hard to believe in melodramatic reports of the Duke's complicity with the Nazis. The Germans knew of his rift with the royal family and Churchill. They also knew that he felt his influence might have averted the war. During the months of June and July they convinced themselves that he might be persuaded – or forced – to come into their hands and dish out statements calling for an end to fighting, and for peace. Following Hitler's victory, he might even be made King again.

'Germany is determined to force England to peace by every means of power,' von Ribbentrop, the German Foreign Minister, wrote in a telegram, 'and upon this happening would be prepared to accommodate any desire expressed by the Duke, especially with a view to the resumption of the English throne by the Duke and Duchess.' To this end von Ribbentrop hatched a plot whereby the Duke would be invited by some friends for a weekend in Spain. Once across the border, he would be detained.

From Spain, government emissaries and friends were despatched to engineer this. Their reports were favourable enough. The Duke was saying that the English could be bombed into submission. From Germany came the SS spymaster Walter Schellenberg to complete the operation. He found the reports exaggerated, but having received Hitler's personal instructions to abduct the Duke he had to do something. To start with, he replaced some of the Portuguese guards at the house with his own. Then, with commendable disregard for his own safety, he sent flowers to the Duchess with anonymous notes warning her of Britain's evil intentions. These intentions were conveyed in full by the Marques de Estella, who talked of a plot to kill them, of the necessity to return with him to Spain. The Duke in turn passed this information on to the British government's trusted go-between, Walter Monckton, who arrived on 28 July. Monckton – known as 'Monkstone' in German intelligence reports – asked for evidence. None was forthcoming.

In the summer of 1940 Portugal was in despair. No one knew whether Germany would continue on into the Peninsula. The place was awash with refugees, spies, 'impoverished grandees and nondescript people, including Rothschilds down to their last two millions'. Even Guy Burgess was there.

What about the Duke of Windsor?

'If you made a list of the people you didn't want him to meet, those were the people he saw,' recalled Hester Marsden-Smedley. 'He had an absolute talent for knowing the wrong people.'

There remains a large question mark over whether he knew any Germans in the summer of 1940. In his book *The Life and Death of Harry Oakes* the recently deceased American royalty watcher Geoffrey Bocca records how Ricardo Espirito Santo 'told me frankly and "on the record" that he had invited the German minister, Baron von Hoyningen-Huene, to meet the Duke. Later, by urgent cables and transatlantic telephone calls, he assured me his memory had been at fault and that he had done nothing of the sort. He died shortly afterwards. Men of sophistication and great international experience do not make such statements to writers without a reason or forethought, and it was a curious error of memory.'

Judith Symington lives close to the house in Sacramento a Lapa which was then the residence of Hoyningen-Huene. In the garden there is a tree planted by Vasco de Gama. Every day, wearing a head scarf and black glasses, she walks her dog down the street. She knows most of what goes on in Lisbon today, and she knew even more then.

'I was driving home one day when I caught sight of a man in the car in front. I thought I recognized him. Isn't that the Duke of Windsor? I nudged my husband. The car stopped some distance from the German residence, and sure enough, it was he who got out. He was wearing a navy suit, and he walked along the street, up the steps and into the house. Obviously he didn't want to be seen. It wasn't the only occasion, either, that I spotted him going to see Hoyningen-Huene.'

'You can mention incidents like that, but there must have been twenty more,' I was told by David Eccles, a diplomat in Lisbon at the time. 'He occupied his days by intriguing. We wanted to get him out. We knew once we had him on the other side of the Atlantic, we could watch him. But if we wanted him out of Europe we had to pay.' He would not talk about the nature of the Duke's intrigues. 'People have been on to me for years about that,' he growled. 'I'm not in favour of the historian's pursuit of truth.' (In his book *By Safe Hand* Lord Eccles restricts himself to a few general remarks about the pair. 'I distrust the Duke of Windsor . . . He's pretty fifth column.' As for his 'beautifully scented' wife, 'I wouldn't give ten shillings for Wallis, she is a poor creature . . . a battered warhorse in a halo hat.')

Cleveland Amory, the American social historian, knew the Duke well, and was asked to write his wife's memoirs. He was not given the job for two reasons. 'I told him I could not make the Duchess into a Rebecca of Sunnybrooke Farm – i.e. an all time sweetie, which is what she wanted as opposed to what she was. And I came up with a title he didn't like. *Untitled*. They really had no humour about their position whatsoever. They were absolutely consumed with petty, almost ridiculous details. With the British army on the beaches of Dunkirk, would she get an HRH? Walter Monckton told me he had the impression they were bargaining with Churchill and if he didn't do something, they would go the other way. I don't think they ever visualized Germany losing the war. I know there were lots of rumours, of the Duke seen poring over maps with Schellenberg, but I don't think he was a traitor. I think he was not very bright, which was difficult for the English people to accept. They like to think their monarchies throw up people with wonderful powers. In this case the water sought its own level.'

Did the Duke have regrets about losing his throne?

Amory laughed. 'Christ, every sentence he spoke began with "when I was King . . . ".'

The Duke played golf at Estoril most days. The receptionist at the club remembered him. 'Multo simpatico,' she repeated, her eyes watering. She showed me his sepia signature in the visitors' book, and the tarnished silver cup he donated, the Duke of Windsor's Cup, given in appreciation of the hospitality he had received there.

While he played, his wife bathed. She missed her favourite green costume though, and asked for the American consul in Nice to fetch it from their shuttered house at La Croë. This he did. A pity he did not send a shirt as well, for the Duke's Comptroller, Major Gray Phillips, was charged with indecent exposure for appearing topless on the beach.

At last, to everyone's relief, an American ship arrived in the Tagus. On 1 August, despite rumours of a bomb on board put about by the ever ingenious – and by now desperate – Schellenberg, the Duke and Duchess of Windsor walked up the gang-plank. Hester Marsden-Smedley saw them leave. 'I remember she had two sewing-machines with her.'

At 3 o'clock in the afternoon, one hour later than planned, the *Excalibur*, recalling the king who had thrown away his sword, departed for Bermuda.

One way of interpreting what went on in Lisbon is to conclude that everyone got it wrong. The Germans were mistaken in believing the Duke might be used as a pawn against the British. The British were mistaken in believing the Duke might go along with this. And the Duke's apologists are mistaken in believing that the British were to blame and that he never set eyes on the enemy. He wanted to do something for his country as much as he wished to have things done for himself. Perhaps he did see the Germans, if only in the hope that he could use his influence on them to end the war, and use the British government's fear of what he was doing in order to get what he wanted.

During the revolution in Portugal of 1974 a watchdog for the ideals concerned was set up, called the Council of Revolution. One of the young captains behind the revolt was put in charge of a special department to disband the dreaded secret police, PIDE. (Policia Internacional e da Defesa de Estado). In the PIDE archives there are files on four million residents in Portugal and her empire, a large proportion of the population. If anything was to be unearthed on the Duke of Windsor's activities, I would find it there.

I was fortunate enough to be in Lisbon at the time when the Thatcherite government under Pinto Balsemao was trying to disband the Council and regain those files. In protest, the Councillor in charge of PIDE's abolition, Major Sousa e Castro, opened them for a day to the press. I missed the occasion – as did most of the journalists, who were on holiday – but was able to persuade the Major to fix another date for me. 'You're lucky,' he said, stroking his T-shirt. 'It's probably the last time anyone will be able to see them.'

At the appointed time I turned up at the offices of the Council of Revolution, a large modern building shaped like a wedge which over-looked a football stadium. Debris remained in the streets from a Roxy Music concert the week before. A black Mercedes was ready to take me to the prison in Caxias, a suburb in the direction of Estoril. Unfortunately the driver did not know the way. He had just been posted to Lisbon from a village in the north. We stopped a cab-driver. 'Just up the hill,' he said. We slowed down beside some joggers. 'Oh, yes. Go down that road,' they pointed. At last we drove through a barrier and braked outside a low grey concrete fort. Through the barbed wire and tall fences there was an impressive view back over the city.

A bulky leather chair in the reception room had a note taped on the back: 'Reserved for the Colonel during lunch hours'. There was a television set opposite. Portugal grinds to a halt at certain times of the day, when the Brazilian soap operas are shown.

In an adjoining corridor, some cleaners were scrubbing the cold floors. They smoked and chatted over their mops. Countless people had been tortured behind the doors which now opened into rooms displaying shelf after shelf of black bound files, each with a pink ribbon. I found the room which houses the index. There is no W in Portuguese, so I flicked through the V's. As I expected, there was no card between Guillerminha Vindombo and Celestino Vindula.

It is possible that the British put pressure on their oldest ally to destroy or relinquish any information on the Duke of Windsor. If so, his secret lies in another file, in London, which contains the correspondence between Churchill, the Duke and the King. It will not be opened for many years.

3

King Carol and Madame Lupescu

Here's to Madame Lupescu
Who came to Romania's rescue.
It's a magnificent thing to be under a King,
Is democracy better, I ask you?

                                        ANON

Two miles from the Boca do Inferno at the corner of a street behind the Lido Hotel is a shuttered villa. It is an imposing place. The yellow walls have greyed and a tangle of ivy darkens one half of the portico. An earthenware pot sits empty beside the steps, but the gravel drive, tiger-striped by the shadows of a cedar tree, is overgrown with plants. The low iron gate is locked and the bell brings no muffled ring from inside. Had it not been for a tarnished plaque bearing the words Mar y Sol, I would not have known this was the last home of Carol II of Romania. He was the next deposed king to arrive on this balmy stretch of Portuguese coastline. Like the Duke of Windsor he too, in his time, had given up his throne for the woman he loved.

Carol was christened after his great-uncle, Romania's first king. An austere, humourless man, Karl of Hohenzollern was a German prince who accepted the crown after the union of the Danubian provinces into one independent state – despite hostility from Austria and Russia. In 1866, with a passport in the name of Karl Hettingen and wearing the requisite pair of goggles, he had taken possession of his new kingdom disguised as a drummer bound for Odessa. 'Now I am a Romanian,' he declared on his arrival, and changed his name to Carol. His wife Elizabeth also became better known under another name, her *nom de plume*. A large woman with a shock of white hair, Carmen Sylva saw herself as an inspired muse. See-sawing between moods of ecstasy and despair, she kept in regular touch with the spirits and during visions would run barefoot through the dew wrapped in trailing drapery. Novelist, poetess, a twelve-stone fairy-godmother to her nation – she called out blessings to her ships through a megaphone – Carmen Sylva dabbled in all the arts. She even forced the Chief Inquisitor to model for a gaudy painting of the Holy Family. When it became clear that she would have no family of her own, Carol named a nephew as his heir apparent.

Ferdinand, a lieutenant in the Prussian army, was a colourless nitwit with sticking out ears, a contrast to his beautiful English wife, Princess Marie, a granddaughter of Queen Victoria, the matriarch of European royalty. Though Marie, with her grey-blue eyes and figure like a poplar, was soon to find solace in many a fine pair of moustaches – 'that English harlot', the Kaiser called her – there was no doubt as to the paternity of her first child. At 1 o'clock in the morning on 5 October 1893 she gave birth to the first Romanian prince to be born on native soil.

As a small boy, Carol was plump, merry and docile. 'Later he became a little pedantic,' according to his mother, interested in rules and laws and all things military. Aged three he would march with a tiny sword at the head of the changing guard, or stand beside the bandmaster with a little stick in his hand. 'Carol likes tiresome things,' his sisters complained, and he was at his most tiresome in the corridor, setting up a customs house so that if they wished to pass by with their toy carts, they first had to pay taxes. Spoiled by Carmen, lectured by the forbidding King and neglected by his parents, Carol grew up under the eye of an English nanny who stood arms akimbo giving everyone pieces of her mind in atrocious French. When Miss Green was replaced by a Swiss tutor with republican and homosexual leanings, the many idiosyncrasies of Carol's ancestors came to the surface. He was to be the scion of his house all right. 'He's like a Swiss cheese, he has so many holes,' lamented his father. 'Six days of the week, Carol is as good as gold – hard-working, conscientious, serious-minded,' his mother observed. 'On the seventh he goes to pieces. Unfortunately, all the major decisions he has been called upon to make have fallen on the seventh day.'

At the outbreak of war in 1914 King Carol died. He had failed to persuade his adopted country to side with Germany. Marie was informed that she was now Queen. 'I have often been asked since what were my emotions when this event took place,' she later confessed, having evidently given much thought to the matter. 'Each time I answered with perfect truthfulness that it was one of the most tremendous and overwhelming emotions in my life.' She used her new position to send her troops to war on the Allies' side. It was a shrewder move than it seemed six months later when the Germans occupied Bucharest and the Romanian Court and army were forced to beat a retreat to the town of Jassy in Moldavia. The Romanians held out until the end of the war, and when Marie visited her dressmaker in Paris she made sure of stopping off at Versailles. On her return home she brought news that Romania had been ceded chunks of Transylvania and Bessarabia which more than doubled the size of the country.

Her son, Crown Prince Carol, had not been idle either. True to the manner of his military education at Potsdam, he had driven to the battle of Maraseti in a white Rolls-Royce. His restricted upbringing had made him truculent, independent and rebellious, so when, on returning to Jassy, he fell in love with a general's daughter called Zizi Lambrino he was reluctant to give her up. In September 1918, claiming the right to shape his own destiny, he announced his intention of marrying Zizi, and renounced his claim to the throne.

Their marriage in a hotel room in Odessa's cathedral church was pronounced illegal and unconstitutional by the Romanian Supreme Court, and Carol was sent to cool off in the monastery of Bistritza.

In August 1919, when he again renounced his succession, Carol began to catch the eye of the world's press. In accounts reminiscent of *The Prisoner of Zenda* he was depicted as a royal prince who had given up all for his Cinderella. The birth of a son, Mircea, in 1920 only fuelled public interest. Under considerable pressure from his parents, Zizi was removed to Paris; and Carol, reinstated as Crown Prince, was despatched on a foreign tour. He hunted tigers in India, continued to Japan, and on his return seemed to have forgotten all about his ex-wife and child. So much so, that in March 1921 he was able to marry Princess Helen of Greece who shortly assured the succession of his dynasty with the birth of a son, Michael. It was not a happy marriage. Carol complained that his pretty, shy wife gave him goose pimples, and they slept in separate bedrooms. Soon there were rumours that he was seeing another woman.

There are several variations on Carol's first meeting with Elena Lupescu, the red-haired, snow-skinned girl from Jassy. Some have her

31

running from the woods when she hears his car, crying 'Help, help! Save me.' Some have Carol struck dumb in 1925 when he sees her walking towards him in the streets of Bucharest. Barbara Cartland, one of the many attracted to Carol's story, opts for an earlier encounter in 1919, at a dinner in Jassy. He falls first for the cooking, then for the cook. At the door, his lips linger over her hand. 'They were both conscious of a tingling excitement . . . Both knew that a message had flashed between them and that they would always remember the sensation which had thrilled them both so that there (*sic*) hearts beat faster and their pulses throbbed whenever they thought of it.'

The lady in question favoured an even earlier introduction. She claimed that, aged nine, she was taken to have tea with the mystic Carmen Sylva. Fifteen-year-old Carol was there too and, stunned by her beautiful hair, commanded the little Lupescu to swallow some chocolates. No sooner had she taken one, than Carol ordered her to pick another. She refused and he grew angry. 'How often we have laughed at that chocolate episode since.'

For twenty years Elena Lupescu was to become one of the world's most talked about women. Though legends have grown around her, little is known of the 'Titian-haired Jewess'. What there is has been clouded by her conflicting, evasive stories. Having created a world of make-believe for herself, a kind of music-hall land of Ruritania, she made things up so that others should believe in it too.

Lupescu's father was a Jew who changed his name from Wolff, quite understandably in a country of virulent anti-Semitism. During the war he had run a small shop in Jassy, the temporary capital, which provided the army with perfume and buttons. For a Jew, the legal obstacles to becoming a pharmacist were insurmountable; he would have needed a high income to pay for his licence, and, more important, several highly placed friends to turn a blind eye to his origin. His daughter's education at an exclusive convent in Bucharest is also puzzling. Its patron was Carol I, and entry was reserved for aristocrats. Elena's marriage to an upper-class army officer called Tampeanu only adds fat to the fire. In the army anti-Semitism was almost a creed. Which makes one turn to her mother, for whom no records exist.

One theory, whispered only in confidential circles, explains all. It features Carol's great-uncle, Carol I. Apparently his intimidating manner concealed a frisky eye for women. While Carmen Sylva waddled through the dew, Carol went a-roving with the village schoolmistress on his royal estate of Peris, a few miles from the capital. He roved so much that she became pregnant, and arrangements were made to marry her off to the village chemist, a man named Wolff. Hence, the story goes, the allusion in a London newspaper of 4 January 1926 to 'a Madame or Princess Lupescu'.

Lupescu – or Duduia, as he engagingly called her – satisfied Carol II's taste for the vulgar. Vivacious, ribald, with a hip-swinging walk, she depended for her beauty on pale skin, wide green eyes and a full mouth, on colour rather than line. A cook of traditional Romanian dishes and a passionate poker player, she was also a woman worth the sacrifice of everything a man holds most dear. King Ferdinand must have had some inkling of this when he sent Carol to London in the winter of 1925 to represent Romania at the funeral of Queen Alexandra. All went smoothly until, on the return journey, Carol stepped off the train at Paris and into the arms of a veiled woman. If was the last his diplomats saw of him.

For the next five years, photographers and journalists were to be his courtiers, writing circulars about his stallion-like appetites, and dispensing titles for him such as the 'Playboy prince' and the 'Royal philanderer'. The name Magda, by which Lupescu became known, started with a report in Milan that she was a bareback circus rider. It was to Milan that the couple now went, and it was there that Carol received a summons from his irate father. Unless he returned without his companion he would forfeit his crown. As his mother added, disentangling herself from the arms of yet another prince, 'One doesn't give up the throne for a Madame Lupescu.' Carol disagreed. He was having too much fun chortling over the chocolate story with his mistress. On 28 December 1925, for the third time in his life, and presumably by now in stitches, he signed a document surrendering all claims to the crown, all authority over his son and pledged never again to set foot on Romanian soil. 'This renunciation is final,' he finished with a flourish. From that day on 'what I desire is silence.'

In her ghosted memoirs, published in 1927, Lupescu sought to correct the image of 'a common courtesan, an unscrupulous selfish siren for whose cheap caresses a Prince of the Royal Blood had renounced the throne.' The reality was far different. Misfortune had flung them together, 'and we clung in a sort of terrified happiness. I held tightly to him as what woman would not in my place for I loved him and am no hypocrite.' But always 'the prying eyes sought us and the cruel tongues went wagging. We so longed for peace and seclusion.' Little effort went into finding it, however.

33

Their wanderings took them to Cannes, Nice, Monte Carlo, and in the spring of 1926 to Paris, where they settled in a ten-room villa at Neuilly. ' "You may go back," I would whisper,' but Carol – or 'Chou chou' as she also whispered – was content to make his bed, dry the dishes and answer the door. He was meek in her presence. She kept him on a tight leash, peeping through a hole in the bookcase whenever he had visitors. When one old friend asked if he was coming back to Romania, a voice behind the shelves cried 'Carol!'

King Ferdinand died in the summer of 1927. Carol was forbidden to attend the funeral, or to witness his six-year-old son, Michael, take up the throne under a Regency Council. Not unnaturally, he began lobbying for a return. 'I have said and I repeat it: if the country calls me I shall answer its call.' Never a man to sit idly by the telephone, he must have summoned a good many sympathizers to his home. No doubt the publication of Lupescu's memoirs was aimed at cleaning up his act. 'I love him so much,' she whined, 'that I would sacrifice my own happiness for his and I would go away, but that would not be a solution to his problems.' No indeed, for she had certainly been their cause.

It is not unlikely that Carol's campaign in Paris came to the attention of the Romanian government. In October 1927 his servant was standing in front of a cinema in the Avenue de la Grand Armée when he was accosted by a woman. Speaking in French, she invited him to lunch at her expense. Obviously a good time was had by all. The man had no recollections of what happened between the end of the meal and the next morning when he woke up in his bed with a splitting headache. He found his personal letters stolen, but two days later they were posted through the letter-box. Only one was missing. It described the daily visitors received by Carol, and included a list of his Romanian adherents in France.

In April 1928 Carol tried to shake such observers off the scent by switching his intrigues to England. Travelling under the name of Mr Jones (imaginative incogniti were never the forte of royalty), he arrived at Oakhurst Court in Surrey, the home of his friend Barbu Jonescu, who had started life washing dishes in Soho. With the backing of the press magnate Lord Rothermere a daring plan was put in motion, code-named Operation Carol. On the morning of 6 May Carol drove to Croydon airfield. Two planes chartered from Imperial Airways were on the runway, their engines revving. They carried a cargo of leaflets to be dropped on a meeting of peasants in Transylvania. The manifesto read as follows:

I shall strive hard to improve your lot and to raise the payment for your hard work. Our good King is dead. Therefore it is my duty to return to Romania and to put our state in its rightful place in the world. I see it as a legacy inherited by me from two great kings to continue their life work through sacrifice, talent and industry. No one can blame me for the ardent wish to return to my son in order to bring him up as a worthy successor of his ancestors. God bless Romania and preserve her from bloodshed.

As Carol neared the gangway a group of men hurried out to intercept him. They were officials from the Home Office, and they carried orders preventing the planes from leaving. Carol returned dejectedly to Oakhurst Court. Meanwhile Lord Rothermere's henchmen made alternative arrangements to transport the leaflets by boat. There was even a scheme to have the courier dressed as a nun. The story went that when eventually the emissary turned up in Romania with his bundle of proclamations, he had not only missed the Transylvanian gathering. He had also fallen among bandits.

The repercussions of this fiasco were felt in the House of Commons. Questions were asked and Prince Carol was informed that his presence in the country was no longer desired. *The Times* saw the incident as a melodramatic stunt out of a Dornford Yates novel – a prince in exile in Surrey, a distant throne, plots in the Balkans, a feminine interest and a whirl of detectives and motor cars. 'If any further proof were needed that he is unfit to occupy the throne he thrice renounced, he has supported it to the full.'

In keeping with proceedings which suggested the vaudeville or the world of film, Carol shortly afterwards took Lupescu to the Stoll Picture Theatre, where they saw *We Are All Gamblers*. On Wednesday 10 May a car with drawn blinds dashed out of Oakhurst Court at high speed and turned in the direction of London. A score of journalists followed at full throttle until the vehicle came to a halt in a traffic jam at Hyde Park Corner. The door was thrown open to reveal an unknown man with two children. All three of them were laughing. Meanwhile Carol had driven to Dover where he was bidden safely on his way, unmolested by the press, by some detectives from Scotland Yard.

The British were not the only ones to declare him *persona non grata*. In June his long-suffering wife, Helen, sued for a divorce on the grounds that he was leading a life 'which is absolutely incompatible with the dignity of marriage'. For the second time the Romanian Supreme Court was called upon to dissolve one of Carol's unions.

Things were by no means satisfactory in Romania. The Regency had fallen into disrepute for failing to unite the provinces. Carol's brother, Prince Nicholas, had taken to chain smoking cigarettes, while another member of the three-man Council spent his time playing patience. The death of the third regent and the fall of the government in November brought things to such a pass that it was thought expedient to make overtures to the exiled and disgraced Prince Carol. Emissaries were sent to test the water, and measure the depth of his commitment to Lupescu. She was to play no part in his return package, for as one dignitary explained to him at the Château de Coesmes, 'You can't make a flag out of a dirty rag.' Loie Fuller, the American dancer who could wind a ribbon of cloth into a dragon of air, was approached at her house in the Chaussée d'Antin and asked to perform a similar miracle. A friend of Carol's mother, Loie suggested buying Lupescu off. She enlisted the help of a Californian sugar-king's widow who it seemed was used to dealing with slippery customers for she kept a python. This woman was willing to pay for Lupescu's flight to British Columbia, as well as her living expenses there. Lupescu feigned willingness. 'The day that HRH is restored to his throne for the happiness of his country, I shall disappear for ever and my only wish is that thereafter no one shall speak of me . . . if it is necessary that I should part from him I am ready to go away from him, even to British Columbia.'

So it was that Carol agreed to return.

On 5 June 1930 he took off from Le Bourget in an aircraft piloted by the French air-ace, Lalouette. After a brief stop in Munich the plane headed east, until suddenly the engine choked, spluttered and stalled. They were out of petrol. Even French air-aces sometimes get it wrong. Dipping below the mountains, Lalouette lost height and lowered his undercarriage over a wheatfield. When he had bumped to a halt, Carol got out. According to his authorized biographer, Baroness van der Hoven, there was a lark singing somewhere in the sky. There was also an old woman in the field. Carol walked up to her. 'Where am I?' he asked. 'Prince Carol? My King!' she is alleged to have replied before wobbling to a pitcher and offering him some water. Shortly after Lalouette had wandered off to find some petrol, another plane came into sight. It was a military aircraft which had been sent to look for him. Leaving the luckless Lalouette and his tongue-tied subject – Carol was a past master at deserting people – he boarded the plane and continued his flight to Bucharest. It must have been galling to find on arrival that there was no one at all to meet him. 'I drove from place to place without finding anyone. At last I decided to go to the home of one man I knew. I actually found him in bed.' When Carol finally came face to face with his son, the boy did not know him. It was a fitting homecoming.

Two days later the 1926 Act of Renunciation was declared invalid, Michael was overlooked and Carol was made King. 'How can Papa be King when I am King?' asked a puzzled Michael. One reason, even a condition, was Carol's promise to seek a reconciliation with his former wife. He at least paid lip service to the government's demand and drove to see her. Refusing to speak to him in private, Helen met him at the head of her staircase. Carol begged her for the sake of Romania and their child to resume married life. She shook her head. He asked permission to kiss her hand. She did not give it.

A few days later Carol informed the Prime Minister, Maniu, who had been instrumental in bringing him back, that he could not live without Lupescu. 'She is the other half of my being,' he sobbed, 'the other half of my life.' When Maniu realized the wool had been pulled over his eyes, that Lupescu had already arrived in Romania (under the name of Madame Manoielesco), he resigned. The following year Queen Helen was ordered to pack her bags.

In his ten years as King of Romania, Carol was to prove a much better monarch than his antics as Crown Prince might have suggested. Which is not to say that his reign lacked absurdities. Once out of civilian clothes he developed a passion for uniform, decorations and all things ceremonial. A short while after his restoration he took a shoe-box of medals to the Pasteur Institute in Bucharest and spent the morning pinning crosses on to the shirtfronts of startled scientists. To symbolize his martyrdom in exile he designed The Order of the Thorn, which was dispensed as lavishly. A new dress uniform was commissioned to improve the prestige of his officers, while he himself took to wearing a large white cloak emblazoned with the crimson cross of Michael the Brave. This preoccupation with form and flourish – as opposed to content – may have stemmed from a case of mistaken identity following his proclamation. The incident has been dressed up many times but it seems to have gone like this. A grand occasion was arranged at which Carol should meet his people. He decided to don the khaki shorts and large brimmed hat of the Boy Scout movement founded by him in 1913 – a movement, with its maxim 'individualism in community', of which he was justly proud. The result was that province after province marched past the royal stand and hailed instead his military aide.

A more serious breach of etiquette occurred in January 1936 during the funeral of George V, who had persistently referred to his cousin Carol as 'that bounder'. The story has it that, piqued at being lodged in a court official's house rather than Buckingham Palace, Carol went on a bender. Next morning, the morning of the funeral, he woke up very much the worse for wear. Resourceful attachés promptly secured the services of a masseur called Mr Stoebs, who at the last moment succeeded in getting the King dressed and into a car. Judging that a final work-out might do some good, he climbed in beside the belching Carol. All too soon he found himself surrounded by marching troops and cheering crowds. Thinking escape impossible, he lost his head. Hastily covering his masseur's apron with some civilian clothes and clad in an ordinary felt hat, Mr Stoebs lined up in the procession and played the part of a lesser diplomat.

The story was wholly concocted by a press that still remembered 'Carol the cad' from his previous trip to England. In fact, the so-called Mr Stoebs was Romania's most celebrated war hero, Constantin Cotolan. What had been mistaken for a masseur's apron was the traditional costume of a Transylvanian peasant. The first Cotolan knew of his role was when he received a telegram promising several thousand dollars to tour the United States.

In Romania Carol made sure that he was treated more seriously. 'I like being King,' he had said, and much good he did in reforming land tenure, making advances in education and shaking up his country's oil industry. Some measure of what he was up against can be gauged by the volatility of his governments: in ten years he was served by eighteen Prime Ministers. He was never a man to hide his disdain for politicians. 'If all the politicians could be thrown into the sea the world would be a better place to live in.'

He also had to contend with the rise of the Iron Guard. Formed after the war to fight Communism, the Iron Guard was a legion of green-shirted militants which received doctrinal stimulus, as well as financial backing, from both Nazis and Fascists. Anti-Semitic by nature, they were led by a mystic and murderer called Codreanu. From his white horse he trumpeted for the 'complete and absolute elimination of the Jews', while from his bed, closely guarded by half a dozen men at attention, he insisted 'I stand for truth and love.' Carol's treatment of Codreanu and his men was similarly inconsistent. He veered from appeasement to open and savage persecution, which only encouraged his political opponents, including the Iron Guard, to unite against him. They were driven together too by their hatred of the person closest to him – 'the Jewess, the she-wolf ', Lupescu.

Lupescu had kept a low profile since her return: she never openly visited the palace, and was never present at Court functions. In fact no one ever saw her: even the car she used had screened and darkened windows. But installed in a modest villa in the Alea Vulpache, she had a telephone by her bed which could reach Carol wherever he was. On one occasion, a young officer gained access to her house, drew a revolver and took aim. Laughing contemptuously, she crossed the room and disarmed him.

Perhaps it was this same gun that Michael saw her brandishing one night as she pursued his naked father down the corridors of the royal palace. Carol was adamant that these were the only corridors in which she held sway. He thumped his desk at any other suggestion. 'Her role is purely that of a companion and friend. She has nothing to do whatsoever with any state affairs or any official function. Her position is purely a private one.' It had public parts, though, and the channel for them was a small, brilliantined man called Ernesto Udureanu. Udureanu had been a mere cavalry officer from Craiova until through his persistence he gained the job of Carol's secretary. Before long he had been elevated to the position of Lord Great Chamberlain, indispensable to both King and, more importantly, his consort. 'I control the King,' he boasted, 'because I control Madame Lupescu.' His position made him one of the most important men in Romania.

However careful she was to confine herself to scene shifting rather than stage appearances, Lupescu remained in a limelight of sorts. There was a furore when her father was discovered to be the man behind the 'affair of the handkerchiefs'. Eager to cash in on his daughter's position, he designed a fawn-coloured handkerchief with a portrait of Carol in each corner. Thousands of these handkerchiefs were distributed to the army. However content Romanian soldiers were to blow their noses into the King's face, they were not so tickled to find the cost of the artificial silk deducted from their pay packet.

They were not being paid very much. As one cavalry colonel told the Minister of Finance, 'I have told my men to pillage and live off the country. I have told my officers to make their charms pay off with rich old women. But what am I to tell my horses to do?' In the general election of 1937 things reached such a point that Carol disregarded the result and summoned a poet to be his Prime Minister. Three months later he dismissed him. He – and presumably Udureanu – had decided that no party could pull Romania together, and that to give power to the strongest, Codreanu's Iron Guard, would mean splitting the country. Instead he formed a one-party government of National Union. Outlawing the Iron Guard and imprisoning Codreanu, he declared martial law. Carol had become an autocratic monarch in what he imagined to be the old style. 'I am master of my country. The government is my government. It must have my approval . . . '

Harold Nicolson, who had lunch with Carol soon after he had made himself a virtual dictator, was impressed by his intelligence and seriousness. Borrowing a top hat and tails and putting a bottle of sal volatile in his pocket to ward off possible attacks of giddiness, Nicolson had sat in a pink plush chair on Carol's right while the King explained his eventual desire for three parties, since two were apt to share the spoils.

The reason for Nicolson's visit was a lecture tour in the Balkans on such subjects as 'Are the British hypocrites?' They certainly proved to be when it came to supporting other monarchies. In 1938 Carol paid a state visit to London, attended spaniel-like by Udureanu who made sure that he had beefsteak for breakfast. He hoped to impress upon the British the vital need to strengthen Romania as a buffer zone to prevent Hitler from bringing the Balkans into his orbit. Having marched into Austria, the Germans desperately wanted Carol's oil and wheat. In return they were prepared to offer cheap toys and aspirins. Chamberlain's government listened and wriggled. The City thought Carol's oil a business risk. The inevitable followed. Under heavy pressure from Hitler, Carol found his economy tied closer and closer to that of Germany. Collaborators trekked across the border posing as tourists and the pro-Axis Iron Guard renewed their subversive campaign of terror against the Jews and Lupescu. Carol's reaction was to have Codreanu shot while trying to escape and to take a break in the Mediterranean on board his ship *Luceafarul* – formerly named *Nahlin*, a boat which had belonged, aptly, to the Duke of Windsor. On his return the Second World War broke out. 'If Romania is attacked by

Charles I's execution, from a woodcut of 1649, sounded the death knell for God's other Deputies on Earth

xiled in England, Louis XVIII ate enough
four and heaved like a ship – often making
ose who met him seasick

His Orléans cousin, Louis Philippe, became
King of the French, but ended his days in
Twickenham growing roses

Manoel II, the last King of Portugal and a great-great-grandson of Louis Philippe. He succeeded on the assassination of his father and brother, but ruled for only two years. In 1910 a revolution forced him off the throne and into exile – which he also spent in Twickenham

Manoel and his German wife, Augusta Victoria, at a horse show in Richmond in 1924. Manoel's main interests were tennis, antiquarian books and playing the organ

Manoel's dominating mother, Queen Amélie, had been born in York House, Twickenham. She remained convinced that the fate of mankind was bound up with that of monarchy

Dom Duarte, Duke of Bragança and present claimant to the Portuguese throne

The house in Estoril of the royalist banker, Ricardo Espirito Santo

The Duke and Duchess of Windsor stayed in Estoril during July 1940. Their one month there was to be fraught with intrigue, but it set the fashion for many other royal families to pass their days of exile in Portugal

Carol of Romania and his dog at Oakhurst Court in Surrey, 1928. 'That bounder', as George V called his cousin, was planning a dramatic flight from Croydon to occupy a throne he had renounced three times

Madame Lupescu, the Titian-haired temptress whom he later married. Her life is made up of incidents that would fit more comfortably into a Dornford Yates novel

Mrs Habsburg Windsor claims to be the illegitimate daughter of George V and Queen Maria Cristina of Spain

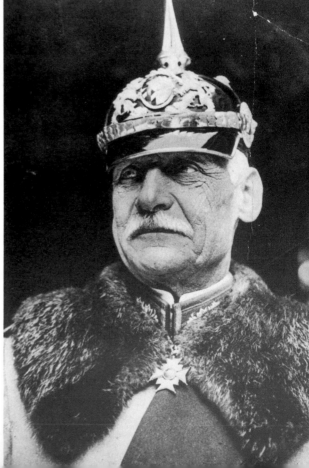

King Rupert of England, Scotland and Ireland – as he was proclaimed by Jacobites. More commonly known as Prince Rupprecht of Bavaria, he traced his Stuart descent from Charles I's daughter, Henrietta

anyone whomsoever,' he declared bravely, if a little pompously, 'she will defend her frontiers and her sovereignty to the last breath.' Thereafter events escalated beyond his dictatorial control. The Prime Minister was murdered. There was another purge of the Iron Guard and, as suddenly, an amnesty declared for its members. Some were even offered posts in the Royal Cabinet. Panic had set in.

Then, in the space of two months, the 'Renaissance King' who had announced that his country would never cede any of her territory to anyone whomsoever, was forced on pain of invasion to give up the province of Bessarabia to Russia, another province to Bulgaria, and to Hungary 17,600 square miles of Transylvania. On 5 September the Iron Guard voiced the anger of a betrayed nation. 'Give us the King!' they bellowed. 'Give us Udureanu. Give us the she-wolf!'

A few minutes after six on the morning of 6 September Carol's ADC emerged from a room on the third floor of the Royal Palace. He carried a sheet of writing paper addressed from the King to his people. It spoke of grave dangers. 'Because of the great love I bear for this country in which I was born and reared, I wish to prevent these dangers by passing today to my son, whom I know you love very dearly, the heavy burden of rule.'

At 3.45 the next morning Carol, Lupescu and Udureanu drove to the Bucharest railway station where a train had been stoked up for two days. It contained hundreds of trunks and cases, one or two servants and five dogs – numbering three poodles and two Pekingese, one of which was called Pussie. 'I can't do without her,' Carol had said. 'She understands everything.' Sunken-cheeked and dejected, Carol climbed out of the car into the rain. He had forsaken his white silk cape for a civilian suit. Hardly noticing the soldiers who presented arms, he stepped into the central carriage. The blinds were drawn and at 4 o'clock sharp the train moved out of its siding.

Few words were exchanged between Carol and his two companions. He smoked cigarette after cigarette as they steamed west towards the Yugoslav border through the wheatfields of Banat. Suddenly an official burst into the carriage with news that a group of Iron Guards was waiting in the town of Timosoara. It seemed they intended to attack the train and shoot Lupescu. She immediately had hysterics. One of the military aides suggested stopping the train and driving Lupescu to the frontier. Sensing unease in Carol's reaction, he added: 'I guarantee Madame Lupescu's safety with my head.'

41

Carol snapped. 'What the hell good would your head be to me,' he roared.

In the end it was decided to follow Udureanu's advice and go full speed through Timosoara. Sure enough as it accelerated past the station, the train was met by a burst of rifle fire. Lupescu's response was to collapse into a bath-tub. Hurling himself on top of her, King Carol II, Prince of Hohenzollern-Sigmaringen and great-grandson of Queen Victoria, left Romania for the last time.

A week later, after a stop in Switzerland, the party reached Spain. They soon found the Iron Guard had no intention of abandoning the chase. In Bucharest Lupescu's house had been opened up and an entrance fee charged, ostensibly for legionary relief. Inside packs of playing cards had been casually stacked to give the impression of a gambling den. Spurred on by Hitler, the Romanian government began pressing for Carol's extradition. They charged him with corruption and malpractice. He was 'a degenerate epileptic and alcoholic, devoid of all morals and principles.' Nazi spies kept close watch on his hotel in Seville, and hostile reports were broadcast from the pro-German radio stations. Under considerable pressure, the Spanish authorities advised Carol that he was not to stray beyond the city limits. Free to leave, Udureanu crossed into Portugal.

Fortunately for Carol, he was not entirely abandoned. He had in Suner, the Spanish Minister of the Interior, an important ally. Suner, who had co-operated in the plot to abduct the Duke of Windsor, owed Carol a timely favour. During the Civil War he had escaped the clutches of the Republicans by taking refuge in the Romanian Embassy. That action had saved his life. He now repaid the debt by suggesting that Carol find his own way out of Spain, and by giving him permission to take motor trips in the country round Seville. Though a car of secret police would always follow, Carol soon accustomed them to a game of run and chase. Combining a passion for fast cars with his Boy Scout's eye for itineraries, Carol would accelerate until he had completely shaken off his escort. Then, slowing down, he would allow them to catch up.

On 3 March 1941 Carol's car again sped out of sight. It was the last his escort saw of him. Having taken note of various short cuts and side roads, Carol materialized at the Portuguese border. There to meet him was the faithful Udureanu.

Less than three months after their arrival in Portugal, the trio were off again. They were not to return for six years. From Cuba they travelled to a suburb in Mexico City, where Udureanu decided to marry a half-French, half-English girl called Monique Cook. From Mexico City, in the summer of 1944, with seven dogs and Monique, they took the road to Rio.

Though he now had a wife to cope with, Udureanu had lost none of his winning ways. One day he opened the door to a man called Mircea. He was Carol's son by his first marriage to Zizi Lambrino and had made the long crossing to Brazil specially to meet his father. 'His Majesty knows no one by the name of Lambrino,' replied Udureanu, firmly closing the door.

Lupescu's celebrated death-bed scene took place in the summer of 1947. Suffering from a severe case of anaemia, she was confined to bed. Carol was told that there was little hope of recovery. Beside himself, he decided to give her the one thing he had until then refused. On 5 July, in the course of a legal service in her bedroom, he slipped a wedding ring on her finger. It was the last of the royal touches. A few days later she had recovered enough to appear again in public. She was greeted as Princess Elena Lupescu.

To ensure her continued health, Carol was advised to take Lupescu to the milder climates of Europe. She repaired to Portugal in the manner of a nineteenth-century invalid. It was the only country to accept her regal retinue, and only did so under pressure. Carol's kinship with the Portuguese royal family may have helped – he was the great-grandson of Queen Maria II – but his good relations with the Portuguese government depended on washing his hands of all political activity. His energies went instead into the purchase and conversion of the Villa Mar y Sol, funded by the sale of his properties in France. Though he dressed in grey flannels and sports shirt, Carol continued to surround himself with an incongruous miniature court. Udureanu resumed his duties as Lord Chamberlain, while another high-ranking refugee was made Master of Ceremonies. Both clicked their heels in public while the ladies of the household made swooping curtsies. Their audience, however, was limited and not particularly appreciative. In fact most of the other royal exiles shunned Carol and his princess. So did the Portuguese aristocracy. Udureanu telephoned the guests for one party at the Mar y Sol and informed them that women would be expected to curtsy to Lupescu. The men turned up without their wives.

Lupescu decided to win favour by courting Catholicism. This after all was the country blessed by the Virgin's visit to Fatima. Lupescu followed in her footsteps, feigning a deaf ear. At the shrine a priest said the relevant prayer. A car hooted. And Lupescu suddenly raised her hands in wonder. 'A miracle!' she exclaimed. 'I can hear.'

Carol meanwhile indulged in the usual pursuits of an ex-King. He pottered around his garden planting gladioli, he pored over his stamp collection and he shot pigeons at a local club. Once a week he took his entourage to that favourite haunt of royalty, the cinema.

The curtain finally dropped on Good Friday 1953. Carol gave a strangled cry and died before the doctor reached his bed. A funeral service was held at the English Church and he was buried at Sao Vicente in the Mausoleum of the Kings of Portugal, his body in evening dress and a cross of the Eastern Orthodox Church in his hand. His brother Prince Nicholas was the only one of the family to appear. 'I came because I felt it was my duty. Although I hated Carol more than anybody in my life, he was my brother and my King.' Lupescu, weeping uncontrollably beneath a black veil, had to be carried away.

It was some time before she recovered. She fingered the things he had touched, she stroked the chairs he had sat in, and she fended off the lawyers who immediately made claims on Carol's estate. Rumours of a fifteen million dollar fortune resulted in the discovery of several hundred dollars lodged in her account, and a ten centime piece in Carol's safe.

Lonely, shunned and impoverished, Lupescu lived on until 1978, attended only by the Udureanus. It was an end without much glamour.

Ernesto and Monique Udureanu live today in the Rua da Beira Baixa, in a house behind the Mar y Sol. They claim Lupescu left them everything. A dog fiercely guards their gate.

Monique was alone when I called. She was a nervous, restless woman who fumbled constantly with a packet of Portuguese cigarettes. The corners of her narrow eyes were made up with lines of black pencil. On the mantelpiece in pride of place was a black and white photograph of her mistress and benefactress, Madame Lupescu. A message in pencil, dated 1943, was scribbled across the neck. 'L'essentiel c'est de vivre pour le retour.'

From the edge of her sofa, Monique told me how her husband had arranged for Carol to escape from Spain. After accelerating out of sight on 3 March 1941, Carol had switched cars and driven to the frontier at Ficalho. 'My husband arranged it all with the help of the Polish secret service. At the border, Carol was met by a Portuguese woman. She was known to the guards and had crossed into Spain on the pretext of seeing a dentist. His Majesty hid in a special compartment under the back seat of her car. When the time came to drive back into Portugal, the head of customs got in, sat on the back seat and personally escorted her over the border. Just think, if he had known what he was sitting on . . . ' Monique added another cigarette to her lips.

'He loved her, you know,' she said after a pause, nodding at the photograph. 'He was always there when she needed something. He was always rushing up to her with his lighter when she had a cigarette.' By now I could understand her example of true affection.

'And that story in Brazil about how she pretended to be ill so he would marry her. It's nonsense, just nonsense. She was very ill. She nearly died. I was there.'

We walked down the hill, to Mar y Sol. Monique found it almost too painful to look at the shuttered villa.

'She left it to me with all the furniture, but the Romanian government are still contesting the will. Would you believe, after all these years? It's so awful. I can't even get inside my own house. They claim there are some El Grecos and a hidden fortune. But there's nothing. And you know they've put it in the care of a man who has an antique business.'

She reached for her handbag. 'It's not surprising it's been broken into.'

The Royal Pantheon is reached through a tiled cloister. The cold stone coffins of the kings and queens of Portugal are piled one upon the other, giving the impression of a bank vault. Over there lies Charles II's widow, Catherine of Bragança. There, next to his mother Amélie, lies King Manoel II, 'que morrer no exilio', as the inscription goes. And by the entrance, chest-high and side by side, are the final resting places of King Carol and his third wife, the only coffins to be covered in thick drapery. They are also the only coffins without an inscription. One epitaph came to mind. Each woman kills the king she loves.

4

The May King

King Umberto, who died in 1983, was the best loved of Estoril's royalty.
To his relations he was 'Uncle Beppo'; to the locals he was one of the
people. His famous chuckle could be heard in fishermen's bars and diplomatic receptions alike. For all that, he was careful to keep his distance from
those he did not know, and it was a long time before I was able to talk to
him. I had seen him at embassy parties, tapping his feet to various
orchestras – on one occasion to a Pink Floyd song, with the line 'You're
just another brick in the wall' – but he was always closely attended by
members of his entourage. My letters requesting an audience received
polite refusals, and lobbying from mutual friends produced no reaction.

As often happens, it took a small thing to change this. I was having
lunch alone one day at the Hotel of Seteais in Sintra when an elderly man
clasping a radio and a copy of the *Herald Tribune* came across to my table.
He asked if I would join him for coffee outside. In the sun, over a brandy,
he revealed himself to be a Dutch philosopher who had lived in the hotel
for twenty years. He was sick of the food, but his room overlooking the
plains allowed him to work out his theory of self-awareness. To the two
notions, the state of being aware and the awareness of the state of being
aware, he had added a third: the awareness of the awareness of the state of
being aware. Analytical dialectics was what he called this novel addition. It

seemed a small return for so much effort. He was capable of more worldly wisdom, however.

'So you want to see Umberto? Well, you won't get very far until you sign your name in his visitors' book.'

That afternoon I walked up the drive to the Villa Italia, a pink house on the Boca do Inferno next to the Duke of Windsor's residence. In the hall, beneath a portrait of Victor Emmanuel III, I added my name to a lengthy list of Italian well-wishers. Some days later I received a phone call from a Count Monasterolo. His Majesty would be pleased to grant me an audience.

King Umberto, who arrived in Portugal in 1946, was the only royal to publicly befriend King Carol and Madame Lupescu. Like Carol, Umberto had an untidy family life. (His wife, Marie-José, spent her exile in Switzerland.) Like Romania, Italy was an old civilization which had not become a kingdom until the nineteenth century. It became so under the House of Savoy, a dynasty of counts and dukes, princes, and – finally – kings who had ruled for longer than the House of David. The tenth-century founder of the dynasty bore the same name as the man who saw its end, and from Umberto the Whitehanded sprang the race of soldiers and mountaineers who were to command the Alpine passes into Piedmont. One of them, Peter of Savoy, became the Earl of Richmond and built himself a palace by the Thames called Savoy House – a site better known today for the hotel, grill and theatre of that name. Not until 1861 was that patchwork of kingdoms and republics known as Italy to be united into a single kingdom under the House of Savoy.

Victor Emmanuel II was one of the few monarchs to find himself on the throne as the result of a revolution. And it was a revolutionary who in 1900 shot his wide-eyed, white-moustached son, Umberto I, after he had handed out some gymnastics prizes at Monza. (He had never been the luckiest of men. The first woman he intended to marry, Archduchess Mathilde of Habsburg, had gone up in flames while waiting for her bath to be prepared. A surreptitious cigarette smoker, she had set fire to her gauze négligé.) 'Remember, to be a king, all you need to know is how to sign your name, read a manuscript and mount a horse,' went the only recorded advice Umberto gave his son, Victor Emmanuel III.

Barely topping five foot, Victor Emmanuel became known as the Tom Thumb of royalty. He needed a stool to mount his horse, and when he ascended the throne in July 1900, it was said unkindly that his feet never touched the ground. His intellectual stature was greater. 'The Prince of Piedmont is the most intelligent prince in Europe,' Queen Victoria had said of him. His study of old coins resulted in the standard multi-volume work entitled *Corpus Numorum Italicorum*. From numismatology, he learned that the currency of kings was minted in battle. Shrimp though he was, Victor Emmanuel became known as *Il primo soldato d'Italia*, the first soldier of Italy. For three years during the First World War he stayed at the front line, photographing his troops in action and distributing food and cigars from his grey Fiat. When the Fascists came to prominence and Mussolini marched on Rome, he refused to sign the order for his arrest. Instead he asked the Fascist leader to form a government. Had not the man declared himself a monarchist, and the throne 'simbolo della patria, simbolo della perpetuia della patria'?

The move saved Italy from civil war, but it lost Victor Emmanuel his footing. He became a cipher, his royal prerogatives disappeared and his toes hung even further from the ground. In 1936, after Mussolini had bellowed from the balcony that Italy was once again an Empire, the new Emperor of Abyssinia returned triumphant to the Quirinal. He was greeted by his wife with boot-polish on her face and a lampshade on her head. 'I am Empress of Abyssinia,' she joked.

On his state visit to Rome in 1938 Hitler was quick to show his distaste for Victor Emmanuel. 'King Nutcracker,' he called him. 'How Mussolini endures it I don't see. I told him again and again to get rid of all this royalty, but he says the time hasn't come yet.' Hitler stayed at the Quirinal in the apartment of Crown Prince Umberto, who was forced to pay for an elaborate bedspread embroidered with the German Eagle. 'Burn the damn thing,' instructed Umberto afterwards. 'I never want to see it again.' But he did. The emblem was to fly beside his country's flag when Mussolini took Italy to war in 1940. Victor Emmanuel had wished for neutrality. Instead, he had to watch the ejection of his troops from Greece, their defeat in East and North Africa, and, in 1943, their surrender in Sicily. In July of that year Victor Emmanuel played a prominent part in forcing Mussolini's resignation. But if the Savoys, as Mussolini charged, had 'executed the demolition of Fascism', they had also assisted in its construction. In that lay their undoing. Only two more knocks were required for the fall of the House of Savoy. Victor Emmanuel supplied them both, with his refusal to abdicate in favour of his son, Umberto, and his flight from Rome.

At 7.45 on the evening of 8 September an armistice was announced between Italy and the Allies. Shortly after 5 o'clock next morning a convoy of cars left the Palazzo Vidoni, the Ministry of War in Rome. Radio Roma was silent, and the Germans had begun disarming Italian troops. The capital was being left in the lurch for the convoy contained both the King and his Prime Minister. Victor Emmanuel led the way in a Fiat 2800. A raincoat covered his grey-green uniform. He had a briefcase for luggage and only 1200 lire on him.

'My God, what a scene,' was the reaction of his son, Umberto, who followed in an Alfa. He had abandoned his post as commander of forces in southern Italy and was plainly worried about the excuse for the journey: to prevent the Eternal City from destruction, and to guarantee the government's continuity in co-operation with the Allies. The convoy drove south through the German forces to the Appenine foothills. By the time it reached the port of Ortona next day, Umberto's doubts had become fears. 'I think I had best go back,' he said. 'I feel it indispensable that a member of my house should be in the capital in such a serious moment as this.' Permission was refused. 'In the House of Savoy,' his father told him, 'we rule one at a time.' At 1a.m. on 10 September, to the sound of catcalls and boos, the royal family boarded a corvette and sailed for Brindisi. The King fell asleep in a deck-chair. His kingdom lay in the dark.

It ill serves a monarch to have his capital surrounded by foreign troops. The French Empire fell when the Prussians reached the gates of Paris, and Parisians – ever conscious of their stomachs – were forced to eat two elephants from the zoo. (Castor and Pollux's trunks sold for 45 francs a pound.)

The Savoys never really had a chance after they deserted Rome. In defence of Victor Emmanuel, it could be said that he left knowing what might happen if the Germans caught him – although they had every chance to do so on his journey south.

Hitler was no respecter of titles. 'What's a Duke?' he had asked on 23 July. 'A small piece of sausage wrapped in the title of a Duke.' He had plans to grill the Savoys following Mussolini's fall on the same day. 'Tomorrow I'll send someone who will pass to the commander of the Third Armoured Division the order to enter Rome with a small group and arrest immediately the whole government, the King and all the other fools; principally to seize the Prince [Umberto] . . . Afterwards, you'll see how gentle and sweet they will become . . . Within eight days I can assure you there will be a nice retaliation.' What Hitler intended to do with them in that time is not known. What is known is the fate of one member of the Savoy family who fell into his hands. On 22 September, twelve days after Victor Emmanuel sailed, his daughter Princess Mafalda returned to Rome from Bulgaria. She had been attending the funeral of her brother-in-law King Boris of Bulgaria (who, it was claimed later, had been murdered on Hitler's instructions by the forcing of a strong blast of oxygen into his flying mask). Hitler regarded Mafalda as 'the trickiest bitch' in the House of Savoy. He ordered her to be arrested and flown to Berlin. She was told that she was being taken to join her husband at the castle of Panker. Instead she was escorted to shed number 15 at the concentration camp of Buchenwald, and given the name Frau Abeba. On 24 August 1944 the Allies bombed this 'school of hard knocks', as Goebbels called it. The Princess was buried under a collapsed roof. Her arm was crushed and she was badly burned. For four days she received no medical attention. The delay was intentional. On the morning after her arm was finally amputated she died of a haemorrhage.

Victor Emmanuel's desertion of Rome was only compounded by his reluctance to break totally with the Nazis – which meant that his troops continued to be bombed by the Allies – and his refusal to abdicate. However much the Italians had accepted it at the time, his association with Mussolini had compromised his position on the throne. The people needed to blame someone for not having opened their eyes. They chose him. The little king had brought the country to its knees. He was the only one it could look in the eye. Not until April 1944 did the Allies intervene. A posse which included Harold Macmillan arrived at the Villa Sangro near Ravelo and asked him to renounce his powers as head of state.

They left with the appointment of his son Prince Umberto of Piedmont as Lieutenant-General of the kingdom. Victor Emmanuel had refused stubbornly to go the whole way. Without any power to go with it, the title he kept did him little good. That winter a naval officer was patrolling the Bay of Naples when he spotted a shabby couple fishing beneath a villa once owned by Lady Hamilton. They were sitting under the windows of the suite where George VI was staying. The officer steered his boat up close and asked them to leave. 'But this is the King and I am the Queen,' replied the irate woman. Opening her bag, she pulled out a visiting card to prove it. It did not matter who they were. 'No one can fish here now,' snapped the lieutenant. 'Go away.'

The sensuous, gallant Umberto was the tallest, most handsome of all the Savoys. His mother, a great hunter of wolves and pelicans, had been out shooting on the day he was born in 1904. He grew up as fit as her, taking gymnastic lessons in the Quirinal gardens, bathing off the village of Gombo, where Shelley had drowned, and visiting the battlefields of the First World War with his father.

Though he had a deep religious side to him, Umberto was also a man of pleasure – and a lavish spender. 'He's a rascal,' his mother said of him. 'He's a real Savoy.' To Chips Channon he was 'charm itself ', but had 'no great intelligence.' His permanent grin on the ski-slopes caused him to be dubbed 'the smiling fool of Europe'.

A cavalier Prince Charming, he also had a touch of the Roman about him. Both sexes were thought to receive his attentions. Indeed, he was having such a good time that when his father commanded him to marry the rich Princess Marie-José of Belgium, he was somewhat abashed. 'I wish I were a fireman so that I could marry whom I please.' They were married in 1930, but within a short time, as with Carol of Romania and Princess Helen, the marriage was effectively dead. Rumours circulated of his affair with the Hollywood queen, Jeanette Macdonald. Dolores del Rio, in hot pursuit, called him 'the handsomest man in Europe'. And at the end of the queue, in low heels and capped teeth, stood Marie-José, who excited him so little that her first two children were born by means of artificial insemination.

Despite a pot-shot taken at Umberto by an anti-Fascist student in Brussels, he was no admirer of Mussolini or the Fascists. On being made Lieutenant-General of the kingdom in 1944 he was quick – unpopularly so – to blame his people for the crimes committed and the defeats incurred by Il Duce. Umberto's actions matched his words. That summer, as commander of the reconstituted armed forces, he had shown the Allies how important it was to have the Italians alongside. The Allies had decided to make an attack on Monte Lungo which was in enemy hands, but they had little information as to how the enemy was deployed. 'They asked the Italians whether there was an officer who knew the place and was willing to go scouting the area. I went. I knew the place very well.' Umberto took off in a small glider, received a spritely burst of German fire and returned half an hour later with the information.

Victor Emmanuel clung to his throne until 9 May 1946. After abdicating in favour of Umberto, and inadvertently misdating the document, he boarded a boat for Alexandria. Standing to attention, he watched his standard being lowered for the last time. He had left it too late. His son Umberto II, King of Italy, Sardinia, Cyprus, Jerusalem and Armenia, and Prince of Busca, Bene and Bra, was to rule for only thirty-four days.

Twenty-three days after his accession, a referendum was held to decide whether Italy was to be a republic or monarchy. The country seemed evenly divided. On Sunday 2 June Umberto's wife Marie-José cast her vote in a polling booth on the Quirinal hill. She voted socialist. Some claim to have seen her tearing down monarchist posters. Umberto had taken to the hustings with vigour. After all, the referendum had sprung from an agreement between him and the government in 1944. 'I decided to make the Italian people choose which institution they would prefer.' It was said he cast his ballot blank.

On 3 June results from the pro-monarchist south indicated a majority for the crown. Next day a landslide of republican votes showed that the outcome would be a close-run thing. In the Quirinal, Umberto stood looking slightly sickly by the green light of his table lamp. 'I'll go by the referendum,' he pledged. 'Italians will always choose the right way. I don't want to buy my throne with money or with blood.' If he ventured out, it was to attend the maimed and wounded children in the Quirinal gardens. (He had transformed one of the villas into a hospital for victims of the bombardment.) 'Sorrida, smile,' a photographer once urged him there. 'Do you think it easy to keep smiling all the time?' Umberto retorted. When the wind changed on 5 June he was not smiling. On that day he heard the republicans had won, by twelve million votes to ten million. 'I think it's going to be a beautiful day,' he said, looking out of the window.

Umberto had bowed his head when told by a friend that defeat in war invariably cost a king his throne. He was unlucky to lose his. The monarchy had become the most convenient scapegoat for everyone's mistakes, so it was hardly the moment to take a referendum. As Romita, the Minister of the Interior, confessed, 'a delay of six months could have been fatal to the republic.' It was a republic born in distrustful circumstances. The government in charge of arranging the referendum was, in its majority, republican and made little effort to protect the monarchists. Armed groups roamed freely in the north, intimidating supporters of

Umberto and accusing them of being Fascist. In May an orderly monarchist procession in Florence was violently assaulted. The police never came to the rescue. In Rome thousands of legally printed leaflets were seized and pavements were daubed with black and white varnish proclaiming 'Morte ai Savoia', 'Republic – or chaos' went the cry, and no one was left in doubt as to the nature of this chaos. 'If the monarchy should unexpectedly prevail with a slight majority,' warned one Communist, 'it would be civil war.'

The confusion that reigned on the eve of the referendum was replaced during it by suspicions of irregularity. There were charges of duplication. In Alexandria, Victor Emmanuel and his wife each received two ballot papers, while many people in Italy were said to have voted more than once. On the ballot paper, the republican symbol was the head of Italy adorned with a tiara. It was an emblem which misled simple people into thinking this was a woman with a crown – and a vote for monarchy. Some ballot papers, it was rumoured, were distributed with a cross already made. If another cross was registered, it constituted a spoiled paper. There were 1,509,755 spoiled papers. That was not all. As Umberto later complained, 'hundreds of thousands of prisoners, countless refugees and the whole population of our province of Bolzano and of the sacred territory of Trieste [occupied by Tito's men] were excluded from this poll.' The total number of people who never had a say in their country's future amounted to two and a quarter million – more than the difference between the republican and the monarchists. Throughout the proceedings and despite these irregularities, the Allies maintained a position of non-intervention. The Italians, they thought, could pull their own chestnuts out of the fire. If anything, bearing in mind the presence of American troops, their sympathies were with the republicans. The royal palace in Naples, where Lady Hamilton had danced with Nelson, was turned into a brothel known as 'the Palace Club'. Looking-glasses were cut up into shaving-mirrors and brocades that had covered the sofas and chairs were reworked into frocks for prostitutes.

Queen Marie-José left for Portugal on 5 June. Umberto decided to wait in Rome until 18 June, when the Supreme Court of Cessation would officially declare the results. On the evening of the twelfth he arrived in a small car at the house of a journalist friend, Luigi Barzini. He was tired out but not bitter. Someone in the room mentioned a Sicilian village. Umberto half closed his eyes and named the villages along the northern coast, one after the other, not missing one. 'And he described some of them, to make us see them again, the tower, the gate, the citrus fruit orchards, the fountain. We had a feeling that he knew all his country yard by yard like this.'

At some point in the evening, Barzini slipped out to the offices of his newspaper. When he returned he brought news that the government had staged a coup and deprived the crown of its powers and properties. Umberto was urged to retaliate, to declare the election rigged, arrest the government and retire to the loyal stronghold of Naples. 'I would not have been lacking in men ready to follow me,' he sadly conceded, but Italians had suffered enough. 'My house united Italy. Going to Naples I would divide it. I do not want a throne stained with blood . . . even if it be Communist blood.' He did not go to bed that night. Next morning, on 13 June, crowds invaded the Quirinal demanding to see him. They reached the antechamber of his study and embraced his knees. 'Don't leave us,' they begged. That afternoon, having shaken hands with some three thousand supporters, Umberto left the palace in a grey flannel suit, carrying a walking stick. 'Last night unexpectedly flouting the law and the independent and sovereign powers of the judiciary, the government carried out a revolutionary move, assuming by a unilateral and arbitrary act powers which do not belong to it. This has placed before me the alternative of either provoking bloodshed or of yielding to violence.' He chose the last. 'Whatever fate awaits our country she can always count on me as the most devoted of her sons.' Thirty-four days after becoming King, and without abdicating, Umberto was driven to Ciampino airport where he boarded a plane for Portugal. 'It remains the saddest hour of my life and every day I remember it.'

As a boy at the castle of Racconigi, Umberto watched the gamekeepers set off each year for Portugal to stock up with pheasants and partridges. 'If you're good,' they told him, 'we'll send you to Portugal to see your aunt.' He recalled the promise on the plane. 'Maybe I've been too good and I'm going to Portugal.'

The weather conditions were so bad that the pilot could hardly keep to his route. At one point he shouted that it was impossible to continue. They should try going back. 'I answered we had to go on. We could not return to Italy.'

Umberto joined his wife and children at the Villa Bela Vista in the Sintra hills. The house had been lent to them by the Marquesa de Cadaval, a woman whose grandfather had been an Italian prime minister and whose family had given seven Doges to Venice. 'It was just a shelter, no electric light, no gas, no heating, no telephone.' Enveloped by the cold wet mist and wrapped in borrowed blankets, they were lost to the world. 'Across the hills my children learned the meaning of the word exile.' According to his doctor, Aldo Castellani (the man who discovered what caused sleeping sickness), Umberto remained his generous, courageous self. Nine days after his arrival, he bumped into a beggar outside the local church. The man had no clothes on under his coat. Umberto gave instructions for a shirt to be brought to his room.

'One of the good ones?' asked his valet.

'Yes.'

'But you only have three shirts, Sir.'

'Never mind,' replied the ex-King. 'This man must have a shirt. I will manage with two.'

By the end of the year the man who had owned forty palaces and as many shooting-lodges managed to find a house on the seafront at Cascais. It was not a happy time. His wife fell ill and after being given a transfusion from the wrong blood group, went blind. She moved to Switzerland for treatment and never returned, settling down instead to write a history of the House of Savoy.

In December 1947 news came of Victor Emmanuel's death in Alexandria. He had only recently been joined there by his daughter, Queen Giovanna of Bulgaria, who had fled from Sofia with her son and not much more than £200. She too came on to Lisbon, where she spends her time knitting.

Victor Emmanuel had passed his year in exile working on his coin collection. In Italy coins bearing his own head were already being taken out of circulation. And his old palace, the Quirinal, before its restoration as the Head of State's official residence, was being rented out as a stage set to an American film company shooting *Cagliostro*. A British film star lay sprawled across Umberto's bed while in the courtyard a group of monarchists in black ties who had come to pay their respects on the occasion of Victor Emmanuel's death were caught up with members of the supporting cast. For a brief instant reality was indistinguishable from fantasy.

In Cascais, where he lived for the next thirty-seven years, Umberto acclimatized himself to a new way of life. 'If it's not easy to be a king, it's far more difficult to be a king in exile. Day after day I had to learn this unrewarding job.' To begin with he found a strange delight in being treated as an ordinary man. He could 'study, travel incognito, spend entire days in libraries and museums, play sports, educate and love my children as any other father without that rigour and distance compulsory to official life which I personally knew as a child and a young man.' In fact, 'my life in exile would be really pleasant and envied if there were not an only regret to sadden it: the impossibility of seeing again, at least from time to time, my country.'

This desire to see his country grew every day. The ban on his family from ever setting foot on Italian soil was brought home some months after his arrival in Portugal. An Italian boat berthed in Lisbon with 300 emigrants on their way to Argentina. Umberto boarded the vessel and shook hands with all of them. The gesture brought a storm of protest from the Italian Minister in Lisbon. Thereafter Umberto took care never to do or say anything which 'could make more difficult the task of those who have the responsibility of governing our country'.

Though he communicated often with his supporters at home, he scrupulously disassociated himself from any political action. The poor wrote wanting him to return as a rich, powerful, merciful king; old dignitaries wrote wanting him to return on a horse with his sword unsheathed; and adventurers wrote wanting him to land on some hidden beach. He did none of these. Instead, on New Year's Day and on the occasion of anniversaries – and disasters – he sent messages of hope and encouragement.

Though Umberto was careful not to identify himself too closely with any of the monarchist parties, he continued to reiterate his faith in the institution he represented. 'I believe in the advantages of monarchy for Italy. That is the only reason why I don't intend to give up the rights of my house. Monarchy is above politics. It is the supreme mediator. It creates sentimental links with the people which make sense of the state. It is like the flag which belongs to all and nobody in particular.' And he cited the kingdoms of northern Europe where parliament continues to safeguard the traditions of freedom.

The 'iniquitous law' of exile compelled Umberto to find other means of discovering his country. He wrote five volumes on the portraits, prints and medals of the House of Savoy. He read Virgil, Montaigne, Goethe and Lawrence, so 'I can also travel to Italy'. He made visits to the Roman remains of San Miguel de la Mota and Cuinimbriga, and in handling a fragment of pottery remembered a time when Portugal was not only at the end of the Empire, 'but also of the world'. Most important of all, he received every Italian who requested an audience.

Umberto became something of a tourist attraction for fellow country-men passing through Lisbon. A parking bay had to be built outside the Villa Italia for the bus-loads who arrived to take snaps of the owner and sign his book. To every Italian of whatever political creed, Umberto came across as a man who hankered for his 'dear beloved country'. 'I think,' said one visitor, 'that every time he parts with one of us, he remembers the instant before his exile.' In parting, to each one he said, 'Would you greet my Italy.'

At precisely five to six, knowing the politeness of kings, I arrived in the bay outside the Villa Italia. It was a quiet evening. No throaty roar from the Atlantic breaking on the black rocks of the Boca do Inferno, just the occasional gurgle. Two oil tankers stood out in the dusk mist. Nearer to shore a returning fishing boat was like an eyelid on the calm sea.

At the door I was greeted by Count Scoppola, a sleek, grey-haired man in a blazer, who ushered me through the hall to an antechamber. The room was hung with flags, a patchwork map of Italy and two portraits of Umberto's parents. Victor Emmanuel and his wife had been staying with the Salisburys on a visit to Queen Victoria, and had given the oils as a gift. On discovering later that the Salisburys had sold them, Umberto instructed friends to buy the portraits back, at any price. 'They gave them to me when they came up for auction. They were very expensive, I think.' Apparently his friends had bid against each other unknowingly, which accounted for the expense.

Through a closed double door came the sound of voices. These continued for several minutes until Scoppola silently appeared from the hall and leant with his ear to the door. At an appropriate moment he turned the handle. Seconds later a large Italian family emerged. It was my turn next.

A man stood waiting in a dark suit that hung crumpled from his thin body. As I bowed, he shook hands, smiling and ushered me with shaking hands into a chair. His smile seemed a permanent feature, engraved by illness rather than joy. When he spoke, he leant into the corner of his chair, rubbing his long fingers together.

To start with, I was worried about the extent to which I could ask questions. It had been made clear that this was to be an audience, not an interview. Also, by a sustained piece of stage management, of closed doors and suspicious counts, Umberto came across as every inch a king. Little daylight penetrated the windows of the Villa Italia, and the magic was, by and large, intact.

'I am a great admirer of your Queen,' he began in a high-pitched voice. 'I saw her lately in the month of April and looking very well.'

Did he then, I wondered, think monarchy had a future?

'Yes,' he answered simply, 'I do.'

I asked about the Duke of Windsor.

'Before I arrived, he lived in the house next door, but then afterwards he came for some years with the Duchess. I saw them often. They rather liked Portugal, and even said once that they wanted a house here. But it didn't work out. There are few royal families left now. When I came there was the royal family of Spain, the royal family of France and my Austrian cousins, the Habsburgs, who had to leave Hungary. So we were a biggish group. And then the Duke of Bragança was allowed to come back to Portugal. Now they've all gone back to their countries, except the Duke of Bragança.'

Was he able to keep in contact with his own country?

'I've got a big office in Rome where all the press is sent. I am in touch with them more or less every day, a lot of faithful supporters, and the newspapers come easily enough to Portugal.'

Every year, he told me, he listened on the telephone to the sound of cheers which sent the horses racing round the town square of Sienna for the Palio. To be banished from Italy was 'very, very frustrating, a very sad feeling'. The bus-loads were some consolation. 'They're all I've got to look forward to.' But Umberto was a man who had spent the last thirty-six years looking back. Every month for him was May 1946. 'I remember it very well, every detail. And I remember very well those who were with me at that time.' He nodded silently, his eyes straying. For an instant the smile dissolved. Then he stood up. Scoppola had opened the door.

Umberto was a sick man for the last years of his life. Originally when he came to London for his Christmas shopping, he stayed at the Savoy, or, courtesy of his former subject, Lord Forte, at the Hyde Park Hotel. Like his doctor in Lisbon, Forte was created a count. Later the King came for treatment at the London Clinic, where he registered under the name of M.

de Sarre. It was on his last visit that he publicly expressed his wish to see 'my Rome, my Turin, my Naples' one last time before he died. The Italian government accordingly put in motion a reform to allow him back as a private citizen.

Ironically, Umberto had become more popular in exile than he was in office. In a country that has the largest Communist party in Western Europe, there is a residual fear of the emotions a monarch might evoke. Mussolini was allowed to be buried at Piedappio, but it was not permissible for the body of Victor Emmanuel to be returned from Alexandria to the Pantheon, the traditional resting place of Italy's kings.

Umberto, the fourth and last King of Italy, did not live to see his land again. He died in Geneva on 18 March 1983, with the word 'Italia' on his lips. His funeral took place six days later at the isolated abbey of Hautecombe in Haute Savoie, where many of his forebears are buried. In Italy it was eventually decided not to screen the ceremony on state television.

It seems probable that the House of Savoy will end as it began, with an Umberto. The throne that sits in a Turin museum is not likely to be occupied by Umberto II's son and heir. Victor Emmanuel IV has not marked himself out to be a man of destiny. He married a water-ski champion instead of a princess and in 1978 fatally shot a young German tourist off the island of Corsica.

Of his three sisters, one is divorced, another is on her second marriage, while the third, Maria Gabriella, has the dubious distinction of having a germ named after her – *Micrococcus viologabriellae*. This microbe, apparently, produces pretty mauve patches when planted on a potato.

5

The French Claimant

'The head of a royal house is permitted to hold one of two ranks, either Commander-in-Chief, or private second class.'

HENRI, COUNT OF PARIS

Until 1948 the most celebrated inhabitant of the village of Ranholas near Sintra was William Beckford. England's wealthiest son and the scandalous author of *Vathek*, Beckford had retired there after being cold-shouldered by those he most wanted to impress: Portugal's royalty and, stranger still, the British Embassy. The only locals to embrace him were the gawky Marquis of Marialva – who could eat two dozen partridges at one sitting – and, less innocently, his son. Rejected by the Court, Beckford surrounded himself, and the boy, with a medley of dwarfs, negresses and warbling castrati. And in the grounds of his *quinta* of Ramalhao, among the hollyhocks and Indian corn, he kept a flock of English sheep.

In 1948 Ranholas became the more conventional home for the French Pretender, the Count of Paris and his family. It was the ban resulting from his aunt Amélie's marriage in 1886 which prevented the head of a former ruling family from entering France. Having fretted on the sidelines in Morocco, Belgium and Spain, the Count now bought the Quinta d'Anjinho. For two years, until the law of exile was abrogated in 1950, he milked his forty cows and tended his 150 sheep – remote offspring, perhaps, of Beckford's flock. Though he lives today in France, his wife still spends part of the year in the grand, green-shuttered house in Ranholas.

One can still see why Isabelle of Orléans and Bragança, the Countess of Paris, was once called the most beautiful woman in Europe. Even now, at seventy-two, she has mischievous eyes and a vivacious way of speaking which draws attention from a body only beginning to show the passing years and the rigours of having borne eleven children. If 'Beppo', the Italian King, was every royal child's favourite uncle, the Countess is certainly their favourite aunt. A great-granddaughter of the last Emperor of Brazil and, like her husband, a descendant of Louis Philippe, she is 'related to the King of Italy, the Barcelonas, the Habsburgs, and the Bragianças . . . ' – she goes on counting with her fingers, but runs out of hands. 'We tried to live in Spain, but it was very shut in. We couldn't get away easily,' she said, bustling me into a room overlooking a garden of palm trees and the sea. She had that way only the French have of making English sound alluring. 'So we came here. It's really the last place in Europe. Exile is really awful. Nobody can know how sad it is to live outside their own country. We were all homesick really.' Portraits of the Orléans family covered every wall, having spent the war in London. One in particular stood out. It was a full-length painting of a man with brilliant azure eyes. He had a yellow scarf around his neck, baggy jodhpurs and a gun. He looked mighty serious.

'The Count of Paris,' she explained.

When he was thirteen Prince Henri d'Orléans – later the Count of Paris – was given dinner by the Bishop of Montpellier, a thin man who talked throughout the meal about Nostradamus. Finally, he stared at the young boy whom he had seated in the place of honour and uttered a prophecy of his own. 'As head of the House of France you will one day bear great responsibilities for this country.' Henri did not have a clue what he was talking about. Before there was any chance of assuming such a position, his two uncles, the Duc d'Orléans (Philippe VIII) and the Duc de Montpensier would have to die without issue. Only then would his father, the Duc de Guise, become Chef de la Maison de France.

Henri's parents were both great-grandchildren of Louis-Philippe. His mother Isabelle was the youngest sister of Queen Amélie of Portugal and the Duc d'Orléans. In true family tradition she had married a cousin in a ceremony at York House, Twickenham. His father, a tall, dry man, was interested, like many of his peers, in archaeology and history. In 1909, a year after Henri's birth, he decided to up sticks for a farm in Morocco where he grew vegetables. After the First World War, in which he served as an ambulance driver and stretcher-bearer, he made more frequent visits to Europe. It was on one of these that his son Henri, as a patient in a Putney nursing home, caught the matron's eye. 'Such a nice young boy, so quiet and studious. You never see him with a novel in his hand, only tomes of philosophy, theology and mathematics.' (The doctor there, who later became physician to King Umberto, gained a different impression on hearing him describe the smelly feet of his parents' courtiers.)

In 1926 the Bishop's prophecy came true. Both Henri's uncles had died without producing children and their claim to the French throne passed to his father. With it came the order of exile, and a move to the Château d'Anjou in Belgium. Now that France was forbidden him the Duc de Guise began to pine for his country. French to the marrow of his bones, he would meet people off the train from Paris but he could never bring himself to see them off on their return journey. When he died, an urn of his capital's earth labelled 'Paris' was buried with him.

While studying at the University of Louvain, Henri went on a visit to the Czechoslovakian estate of his nineteen-year-old cousin, Isabelle of Orléans and Bragança. He came under her spell while out hunting. 'If a roe-buck had come and bowed to us, we wouldn't have noticed.' They rode back from the field engaged. One month before their marriage, in March 1931, Isabelle went to Paris and stood for two days in her wedding dress at the Hôtel Lambert while French monarchists filed past. One peasant, who remembered the Emperor Louis Napoleon, had walked forty miles to see the new Dauphine. The only person who could not see her, her fiancé, waited in their new home, a castle in the Ardennes. From the battlements of the Château d'Agimont, he looked bleakly on to France.

The Duc de Guise was more interested in his studies than his position as keeper of the Royal Flame. He spent weeks at a time alone in his study with military history books. In his father's name Henri began to turn the cause of monarchy, and his eventual position as Pretender, into a profession for himself and a political solution for France.

As one friend observed, 'Prince Henri is starting from zero.' He had handicaps enough, but his greatest, ironically, came in the shape of his most ardent supporters, *L'Action française*. Founded in 1899 by the quasi-Fascist Charles Maurras – who in 1945 was imprisoned as a collaborator – this movement was more nationalist than royalist. It sought to restore the grandeur that was France, and attempted to do so in ways that resembled a later movement in Britain, the National Front. Condemned by the Papacy, *L'Action française* nevertheless became associated in the public eye with everything Henri stood for – regardless of the fact that he soon repudiated them. 'The House of France alone,' he warned, 'is qualified to define what the monarchy of tomorrow shall be.'

What he stood for was to be disseminated in two weekly papers founded by him in 1934, and an essay published in the same year on the government of tomorrow. In it he stressed that a king, even a would-be king, could not afford to be a man of any party. He was to be 'le roi de tous les français', an arbiter who incarnated the nation and symbolized its permanence and continuity. 'I have no illusions as to the magnitude of the task,' he later wrote in language reminiscent of the Count of Chambord, who had forsaken his throne for a flag; 'and I am deeply convinced that I shall succeed. We shall reach, I am certain, the great avenue of final triumph.' (Much later he was to confess, 'I have perhaps sinned by an excess of confidence.') In order to encourage men up this avenue, special medals were awarded as proof of service and an ABC guide was circulated to allay the more fundamental fears of non-believers.

'And if the King is mad?' asks a sensible Janet-type citizen.

'It has happened once in 800 years with Charles VI,' John is quick to assure her. 'In a case like that there is the Regency . . . '

'And if the King is mediocre?' Janet persists.

'Then it's in his interests to surround himself with men who aren't,' replies John, a little testily.

'How will he be able to do that?'

'Because he has been initiated from early on by his entourage and educated in the affairs of state; because being a king by profession, he has that flair.'

Nineteen thirty-eight was billed 'the year of penetration'. At the Château d'Agimont, in front of a large map of France, the Count of Paris faced an English newsreel camera. The features of his narrow face were sharpened by a V-shaped moustache and oiled black hair. His eyes were piercing as he began his prepared message:

'French monarchy will restore order and authority and will protect the principles of Christian civilization, justice, brotherhood and human dignity. These principles have been denied by dictators in the name of totalitarianism and racism carried to all excesses against which I do protest with all my energy. Thus French monarchy will stand by the side . . . '

The camera cut. He had slurred his words, pronouncing monarchy as 'monarchee' and denied as 'denided'. He stroked his hair and began again. 'French monarchee . . . ' A few seconds later there was another retake. He had said 'dictatures' instead of dictators. Once more he set off, a little more nervously. 'Against I do protest with all my energy.' No good. 'Zut!' he laughed, his eyes twinkling. He tried again and this time got to the end. 'Thus French monarchee will stand by the side of democracies.'

It is unfair to make fun of a man trying to speak another language, but in political terms that is precisely what he was doing, and it gives some idea of how the average Frenchman saw him then: at best, as a man who represented an ideal that belonged to the past; at worst, as a slightly comical stuntman.

This impression was confirmed when, in the autumn of that year, incensed by the Anglo-French agreement at Munich, he made a brief foray inside France. Representatives from fifteen newspapers had been given detailed instructions to assemble in a northern village where the Countess of Paris would appear to deliver a message. To their surprise, the small plane that landed in the Normandy field contained the Count himself. After posing for photographers, his hair flying in the wind, he called on France to restore the monarchy and end what he described as her period of weakness. Then, reminiscent of one of the Marx brothers, he strapped himself into the cockpit again and flew back to Belgium.

When war broke out, the Count of Paris was refused permission to join the French army. He tried, via George VI, to enlist with the British forces, but the King would not give him an audience. Delighted to hear from him, of course, 'but I am sure you will understand how busy I am these days.' The French government finally entrusted him with an unofficial diplomatic brief, to find out what Europe's royalty, including Victor Emmanuel, intended to do about Hitler. The mission proved fruitless – they could do nothing – and after more persistent requests he was allowed to enter the Foreign Legion as a private. There was one condition. He had to work under an assumed name. A few months later, having spent his time in full retreat, he was demobilized. Hard on the fall of France came news that his father was seriously ill. He managed to get a passage to the family home in Morocco, but arrived too late. So it was that on 25 August 1940 Monsieur Henri Orliac, a Swiss citizen, became Henry VI, the fifth French King in exile.

He spent the war with his family at Larache in Morocco, urging Frenchmen to resist the Germans 'by all possible means'. He still saw himself as an arbitrator, and when a plea came from the Free French to join de Gaulle in London, he never responded. He was above factions, and therein lay his undoing. 'Had the Count of Paris joined me in London in 1940,' de Gaulle could safely say afterwards, 'he would have become France. Together we would have done great things.' Instead he hoped to do great things in French North Africa. It seemed a much more certain proposition to David Eccles who had moved from Lisbon to Tangier. 'The most obvious move would be for the Comte de Paris to declare himself King of all Frenchmen, to do it in Algiers and to couple it with war on the Germans.' Ever anxious to have the consent of the people, he never made this *coup d'état*. He preferred to acquiesce with various movements which sought to elect him legally. They came to nothing.

After the war Henri moved briefly to Spain before settling in Portugal. Both politically and geographically, with its face to the seas, it was a more open country, and the Salazar government was on good terms with both the British and the Americans. And of course he had relations there in much the same boat.

By now Isabelle had given birth to eleven children. Had she produced a twelfth the President of France would automatically have become its godfather. The little tribe went to school in Lisbon, walked to Fatima in straw hats and shot the rats that ate the bindings of their father's books. In his Arab trousers, Henri toiled at his desk – founding yet another newspaper, the *Bulletin Mensuel* – and pressed for the French government to let him back, to change the law which was punishing his family for a crime none of them had committed. 'I burned with a desire to tread again on French soil.' He compared the exile to a deaf man whose 'only dream was to correspond, to listen and to speak'. Like King Umberto, he loved his country with an intensity few patriots possess. 'Before he is a Prince, a Prince of the House of France is a Frenchman. He suffers more from the fatherland's misfortune than for the impotence to which he is condemned.

In the summer of 1950 the law of exile was at last abrogated. Twenty-four years after being banished, Henri was allowed to come home. 'For my return I resolved to take the exact route, but in reverse, that my grandfather had taken when he left for exile.' In doing so he wanted to cancel out the last sixty-four years. On 5 July, together with Isabelle, he took the channel steamer from England to Calais, and the road to Paris. After thanking President Auriol, they drove south to collect their children. On the way, in a Breton village, a woman served them with a delicious almond cake. Appropriately enough it was called 'the exile'.

Henri had never given up hope in exile. He did not intend to compromise himself now. 'By returning to France,' he warned, 'I am renouncing neither my ideal, nor my political role.' In de Gaulle, he thought he had found a man who could help him. From their first meeting in 1954 they entered into a regular correspondence. At the wedding of Henri's eldest son in 1957, de Gaulle wrote a warm message of congratulation. 'Everything you stand for at present is exemplary and as far as your future and that of Prince Henri are concerned, they are integrated in the hopes of France.'

After supporting de Gaulle's successful run for the presidency in 1958, Henri saw much more of him. From their discussions at the Elysée palace he drew further encouragement. On the question of monarchy they had 'des conceptions semblables'. 'I insist that he was more willing than I was to use the word King and that he did not exclude the possibility of a restoration founded on divine right . . . he thought monarchy was the form of government most adequate for the French under the present constitution.'

Henri's concept of monarchy had matured since the 1930s. Though he remained above politics, he realized that monarchy was nevertheless a political institution. The institution he advocated became increasingly left wing. In the *Bulletin Mensuel* he tackled the social and economical inequalities that were crippling France. He favoured the nationalization of all public utilities. He argued for a more democratic involvement of the people in reaching a solution. 'I am a Capet,' explained this descendant of Louis-Philippe, the bourgeois King, 'and the Capetians have always been on the people's side against feudalism.' On another occasion he called himself 'the man most capable of saving republican ideals'. Others styled him as the Crown Prince of the Republic, one observer going so far as to say that his ideas blended exactly with those of Mitterand.

Though he was accused of supporting the left and spurning the right – who would support him anyway – Henri was at least taken more seriously than before. In 1956 the Socialists sent him abroad as a delegate. In 1961 de Gaulle despatched him to North Africa and the Middle East and in 1962 he was summoned to the Elysée with the prospect of an even greater post. On 18 December, in spite of the cold, de Gaulle waited for him on the steps. According to Henri he announced an intention to finish his seven-year term of office, 'then let me run'. 'You have three years to prepare yourself.'

Henri never succeeded as President of France. In 1964 de Gaulle changed his mind and ran himself. Three years later Henri gave up politics and closed down his Bulletin. He now runs two institutions which look after old people and ancient monuments – things, like himself, of the past.

In his memoirs de Gaulle devotes a single paragraph to the Count of Paris. From the discreet meetings with the punctilious heir of kings, he gained, he wrote, 'profit and encouragement'. There was no mention of the presidency. To an aide he confided that Henri did not belong to the age. 'In our age, monarchies are not made. They are unmade. . . . What count in politics are realities. . . . The Count of Paris hasn't a chance.' Perhaps his ideas were too democratic and radical. He would have made an excellent republican, one commentator said, if only he wasn't so far to the left. Perhaps de Gaulle never forgave him for not joining the Free French in 1940. In the end he may have failed because however political his envisaged system, he never allied himself to any party.

Henri's house ruled France, with a break or two, for 900 years. The gap of 135 years since 1848 is a short interruption by comparison. His consolation lies in the knowledge that good cooks do not waste yesterday's soup, and that the word impossible, as Napoleon said, is not a French word. Nevertheless, barring a major upheaval, the only presidency that the Count of Paris is likely to get is that of the Twickenham Rowing Club.

Portugal is a land of earthquakes. Today the tremors are not so violent. They last a few seconds and leave a crack in the wall – and the wall intact. After one such tremor in Ranholas, the Countess rushed everyone out of the house. Only one guest, Ricardo Espirito Santo, was missing. She hared back inside and found him calmly helping himself to some cold meat in the dining-room.

'Europe is in such trouble everywhere,' said the Countess of Paris as we stepped on to the terrace overlooking her garden. She had not felt so worried since the last war. 'Perhaps in a few generations the political situation will be something different. I am sure that it will change but I don't know when. I think now is not the time,' she confessed reasonably, alluding to a restoration of monarchy in France. 'Maybe for my grandchildren.'

It is them she worries about. In every sense she is a family woman, and with thirty-nine grandchildren it is a large family. Shopkeepers have been known to offer a discount, mistaking Henri for the headmaster of a seminary. While he went off 'like the wind' to France and Morocco, she stayed with them, spending more and more time in Portugal. The worst moment came in October 1960. She was telephoned with the news that her second son François had died in action in North Africa while going to the help of a wounded man. A minute or so later she heard her husband arrive. She went to meet him in the hall. On opening the door and seeing her face, he said 'François'. 'Yes,' she replied. 'The greatest sorrow of our lives in those two simple words.'

A car hooted from the other side of the house. She threw her cigarette on to the lawn below. She was sorry but she had to go and join the Misericordia procession in Sintra. Every year a statue of the Virgin was carried from the village church to the royal palace. It was part of her function as the president of various fêtes and charities. Before she left, she gave me a copy of her memoirs. 'For Nelson Schacksepere', she wrote. (Spelling was never a Bragança forte.) In the courtyard an old Portuguese lady had come to collect her. They drove off in the battered car tooting at everything in sight.

6

Sebastianismo

'A monarch has to pay for the mistakes of a dictator.'

ALEXANDER, GRAND DUKE OF RUSSIA

When visiting Portugal today it is hard to imagine that this little country was the home of sailors, soldiers and missionaries who in the sixteenth century discovered, ruled and converted the world. In a sense Portugal has stumbled backwards into the present with her eyes still fixed on those days of Empire. She has never recovered fully from its loss, nor in its heyday from the loss of her King Sebastian.

A mystic with a droopy underlip, Sebastian had heard voices and seen visions which led him to believe he could drive the Moors from Morocco. Until 1578 he had only shot wolves in royal parks, but in that year he took off with a large expedition to subdue the Saracen. He never returned. The outcome of the battle of Alcazarquivir was a fiasco. 'A king,' he was last heard crying as his third horse fell under him and he mounted a fourth, 'surrenders liberty only with life!'

A country without a king was too good a bait for Spain. Two years later she conquered her rival, to rule over Portugal until 1640. It was not a quiet possession. Rumours spread fast that Sebastian had never died in battle, that he would return to save the nation. Sure enough, twenty years after Alcazarquivir a man answering to his name was discovered selling pies in Padua. He had, he claimed, escaped from the battlefield and gone on a world tour. After meeting Prester John in Ethiopia, he had been bought and sold thirteen times, had helped the Persians fight the Turks and dallied a while with the Grand Llama in Tibet. In 1597, however, he began getting visions which admonished him to go back to Portugal and take up his crown. The Portuguese were delighted. (According to one chronicler,

71

'they would have acknowledged a negro as their lost king' – so long as he delivered them from Spanish rule.) The Spanish were less enthusiastic. They arranged for him to be thrown into a Venetian jail pending the outcome of an inquiry. Two things worried them. Whereas Sebastian had been fair, this man had a dark complexion. And he did not speak much Portuguese. The commissioners, however, found bodily peculiarities which Sebastian was known to possess: a right hand larger than the left, a scar above his right eyebrow, and 'a large excrescence or wart on the instep of his right foot'. It seemed after all that this was the rightful King. The Spaniards could not afford to agree. They had him paraded through the streets on an ass, put him in irons and condemned him to the galleys for life.

The belief that Sebastian, like Arthur, would come again, did not die with him – or his impersonators (there were, incidentally, three more). Centuries later, the movement known as Sebastianismo was alive and well and flourishing in small villages of the Alentejo, where even today one may hear his name spoken.

In 1640 the Lisbon nobility revolted and proclaimed the Duke of Bragança their King. He was a descendant of the Capetians of France and founded a dynasty which ruled Portugal until 1910.

When Manoel II died childless in 1932, his claim to the throne passed to a cousin, the Duke of Bragança. Until 1950, if the Duke, his wife – the Countess of Paris' sister – or any of his family were found in Portugal, they could legally be killed. But in that year, which saw the Count of Paris back in France, the dictator Salazar discovered that the law of exile had been illegally drafted. Besides which, after inviting all sorts of other royalty to settle near Lisbon, he could not very well exclude his own house. He allowed the Braganças to return but, penny-pincher that he was, he did not return to them their considerable wealth. They arrived from their small Swiss villa more or less destitute.

The Duke stayed briefly in the Estoril house of a supporter before settling near Coimbra. He grew cacti and carried a transistor radio with him everywhere he went. He never met Salazar. In common with most dictators, his views on monarchy were, to say the least, ambivalent. When the Portuguese ambassador in London invited the Duke to dinner – he was calling on George VI – Salazar had him recalled. 'It is not well to have men chained to corpses.' Yet as de Gaulle and Franco made their respective overtures to the French and Spanish claimants, Salazar seemed to change

Victor Emmanuel III of Italy saluting at a review (above). To be a king, his father told him, you needed to know how to mount a horse. Known as the Tom Thumb of Royalty, Victor Emmanuel required a stool to do this. It was said unkindly that when sitting on the throne, his feet never touched the ground

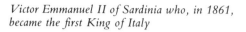

Victor Emmanuel II of Sardinia who, in 1861, became the first King of Italy

Umberto II, the last King of Italy, at the Vill[a] Italia in Portugal shortly before his death in 1983. Known as the May King, he ruled for little more than the duration of that month in 1946

*Crown Prince Umberto with his fiancée, Princess Marie-José, before their wedding in 1930.
He wished he could have been a fireman, free to marry anyone he chose*

Isabelle of Orléans and Bragança, the Countess of Paris (left, in 1940, and above, in 1983).
Wife of the claimant to the throne of France, she was once known as the most beautiful woman
in Europe

The Count and Countess of Paris at their desk in Morocco, 1940

His ancestors numbered Kings of France and a President of the Twickenham Rowing Club. Henri d'Orléans, Count of Paris has put his own considerable mind to becoming variously a British soldier, King Henry VI and a President of France

Emperor Charles of Austria-
Hungary at his coronation in
Budapest in 1916, with his wife,
Zita, and four-year-old son, Otto.
The cross on the crown of St
Stephen was bent during a
robbery

Archduke Otto in the uniform of
a general of the Hungarian
Hussars. As a young boy his shoe
laces were always undone. 'One
must never make knots,' he
explained

Archduke Otto – or, as he prefers, Dr Habsburg – stranded rather forlornly at the Austrian border in 1964. Banned from Austria since 1919, he was not given a passport allowing him entry for another two years

his tune. In 1957 he paid tribute to those who 'led the nation through eight centuries of history'. More significantly, he took the 'prudent view that there may come a time when the monarchical solution is the national solution.' Experts felt he would restore the monarchy at the same time as the Spanish. They were wrong. He retired in 1968 following a stroke – seven years before King Juan Carlos succeeded Franco. He had still not met, least of all groomed the man who would now be King of Portugal.

When the Duke of Bragança died in 1976, his title and claim passed to his eldest son, Dom Duarte, who had recently returned from military service in Africa. 'He is almost more African than European,' his father had said of him. Was he the long-awaited Sebastian?

Dom Duarte, Duke of Bragança, lives alone in a seventeenth-century house near Ranholas in a village called Sao Pedro da Sintra. The bells in the fire-station opposite are always going off. There are frequent forest fires in these hills, lit, it is thought, by the Communists.

When he joined me in a large bare drawing-room, I recalled his fine moustache and flat red face. He offered me a glass of port; the bottle said simply 1915. As I found out, he had lost himself comfortably in the past, and he talked a lot about it, clearing his throat now and then with a nervous cough. He came across as both aristocrat and rustic.

Dom Duarte laments not only the loss of his country's sixteenth-century empire, but also, more recently, the Portuguese possessions in Africa – 'the provinces'.

'I was in the air force four years as a helicopter pilot, evacuating the wounded in Angola. But I also used the time to visit the whole territory on a motor bike. If Portugal was a monarchy what occurred in Angola and Mozambique would never have happened. I think some sort of common-wealth solution could have been found. And we would never have had the catastrophe of 1974–5.' After the 1974 revolution Portuguese African territories were granted independence. 'They were given up to local Communist parties without any election, any consultation with the local people or the Portuguese. With one million refugees, it meant a catas-trophe for Portugal,' he repeated with a cough. He was a man much given to repetition. 'All this could have been avoided.'

In his Lisbon office, Dom Duarte runs an agency that rehabilitates these refugees in South America. 'I will never cease to regard you, my brothers of the Lusitanian idiom, with . . . immense affection,' he promises as they pack their bags for Venezuela. 'I look at you and the Portuguese nation as indissolubly linked.'

Whether Portugal enjoys the same ties with fellow refugees like himself is not clear. Was he more than a kind of national mascot, or was he a dog with some bite? I found an answer of sorts in the hall as he proudly showed me his gun collection – a cabinet of blunderbusses and long-barrelled shot-guns. 'This,' he said, extracting a metal walking stick made in London, 'belonged to King Carlos.' He pressed a catch to reveal a bullet chamber and trigger. Lethal though this shooting stick was, it had not helped save the King. 'He had it with him when he was assassinated . . . ' The rest was drowned by the fire-station bells.

Dom Duarte is not only a philanthropist and businessman – he runs an agricultural co-operative, a kind of farmers' bank – he is also a curator. Like his uncle, the Count of Paris, he works hard for the protection of national monuments, and it was the greatest of these we now drove to see.

Pena Palace rises dramatically from the highest of Sintra's hills. It was built on the site of an early monastery, in a style that has as many strains as the Braganças. Gold Arab roofs and gothic turrets clash with High Victorian motifs to make it the apotheosis of kitsch. If the Duke of Bragança were king this would be his home, and from its discordant terraces, over the wild park where the rarest of plants seem to thrive, he could survey his kingdom. On a clear day, you can turn slowly and trace the coast from Lisbon, the 25 April Bridge, to Estoril, Cascais and behind you, in the hazy distance, the fishing village of Ericeira. Unfortunately, there are few clear days. More often than not Pena is shrouded in damp mist, as it was that afternoon. We could not see a thing.

'I would never live in a place like this,' Dom Duarte said, buying a postcard of the palace. He had not visited Pena for some time. He waited in a queue behind three tourists who wore 'Royal Tour' badges. 'You'd only get rheumatism. Sometimes the only cloud in Europe is sitting over this castle. I like it much better where I am now.'

Dom Duarte is a private man who avoids publicity. 'It is not for royalty to impose itself,' he says, 'but to be aware of the call of the people.' He keeps a low profile, but is so keen to remain above politics that, living as he does in the Sintra clouds, few people are aware – or impressed – by his existence. 'I once tried to join a sporting club in Lisbon, and in the form they gave me, under occupation, I put chimney-sweep. It was what I was doing at the time. They wouldn't have me.'

The Count of Paris has a political system but no party. The Duke of Bragança is endowed with the opposite. In 1982 the PPM, the Monarchist Party, was the third strand in Pinto Balsemao's coalition government. The Monarchists had three secretaries of state and one minister, the minister for the Quality of Life, who for a fortnight stood in as Prime Minister.

Luis Coimbra was one of the republic's six monarchist MPs democratically elected to parliament. (There has since been an election with a different result.) I called on him at the Assembly, threading my way through a band which was playing in honour of a visiting Italian dignitary. Few people were watching. Coimbra, who once worked for Hawker-Siddeley, is a small man with a large moustache – the hallmark of Portuguese men. Though his party's programme was mainly ecological in nature, Coimbra was nevertheless keen for his candidate, the Duke of Bragança, to resume the throne. 'Since the republic in Portugal, we've been going down the drain,' he said candidly. 'Why should we have in politics a situation that no one would tolerate on the football field? The crowds don't accept a referee who is elected by the team with the biggest number of supporters. And that is what the king would be, a referee, above politics. He must obviously come from history.'

Despite the fact that the Monarchists had only 6 per cent of the official vote at that time, Coimbra believed it was everyone's second party. He explained how a particular town in the north was a no-go area because a PPM policy had been delayed in parliament and the people were furious. And, he asked me, with a laugh that had an edge of seriousness, had I heard about the 1 April newsflash on Portuguese television and the item about the government's decision to restore the monarchy? 'The switchboards were jammed with people offering to help.'

It made economical as well as political sense. A monarchy was the cheapest form of state, argued Coimbra, and it brought in the tourists. Look at Buckingham Palace. Who met a visiting president to Portugal? No one. But when the Queen and Prince Philip paid a state visit in 1957, people had never heard such cheers. (It seemed to Prince Philip a kind of hunger.)

I wondered how Coimbra planned to make an April fool's joke reality. 'We think we can achieve monarchy by means of a referendum,' he answered. (The left-wing President Eanes, an ex-gymnastics instructor, told another man I met that, in the case of a referendum, 'you can count on two votes in this house' – meaning himself and his wife.) Was such a referendum likely? 'If the Duke of Bragança marries a princess,' Luis Coimbra promised, 'it will be a walk-through.'

If that is the sticking-point, it is a problem. The Duke's father insisted he should marry into a noble family. It was the only way to breed thorough-breds, he said, comparing royalty to racehorses. The trouble is, there are not so many spare royal fillies prancing around Europe.

'I told him marry a relation. But he's worried about consanguinity. I told him consanguinity does not necessarily make cuckoo people.' The speaker was his aunt, Princess Teresa of Orléans and Bragança. The occasion was a lunch with the Marquesa da Cadaval, the owner of Byron's house in Venice. The venue was her house in Sintra across the road from where the King of Italy had first lived.

Princess Teresa – or Teti as she is known – is the Countess of Paris's charming, irreverent sister. She has the same blue, twinkling eyes, and a hairdo like the plumage of a rare bird. Would she mind whom her daughter married? 'No, I would not mind,' she replied, smiling. 'I would prefer her to marry a man, though.'

Relations between the exiled royal families in Portugal can be often curt, but this serene, baroque Princess – the sanest of them all – is permanently made welcome. 'I am always on the road,' she laughs, and then tells me at a pace of the movement to make her claimant to the Brazilian throne. 'My great-grandfather, the last Emperor of Brazil, abolished slavery, and look at me now. A slave.'

Princess Teresa does not share the reticence of her relations in speaking about each other. She recalls a tiff with King Carol's ADC and his wife, how they cast doubts on her honour at a nightclub in Rio. She complained to the King. Next day the pair of them came and sheepishly apologized. She talks of Umberto, how he had never said a bad word about anybody. And suddenly she comes out with a confession that could be the secret to every one of these people. 'You know, I go to bed each night thanking God there are so many snobs in the world to keep us around.'

PART TWO
THE EMPEROR'S NEW CLOTHES

7

Mr Europe

'A king in exile learns to forget and to forgive almost anything.'

ALFONSO XIII OF SPAIN

The biggest fish to wash up on the shores of Portugal arrived long before the Second World War. In 1921 the British cruiser HMS *Cardiff* sailed Emperor Charles of Austria-Hungary to exile on the Portuguese island of Madeira. Earlier that year, in two disastrous bids for power, Charles had entered Hungary. It was the only part of his former Empire which constitutionally remained a kingdom. On both occasions he was repulsed by the man who had assumed the powers of Regent in his absence – a man, moreover who had sworn an oath of allegiance to him – his former Admiral, Nicholas Horthy. At thirty-four, Charles was a broken man. A few months later, in the Quinta do Monte above Funchal, he contracted pneumonia. As the condition worsened, he ordered his ten-year-old son Otto to his bed. 'The poor boy,' he apologized. 'But I had to call him to show him an example. He has to know how one conducts oneself in such situations, as Catholic and as Emperor.' Four days later, on 1 April 1922, the last of the Habsburg Emperors, heir to the Holy Roman Empire of Charlemagne and the Caesars, died penniless and blue-lipped with fever.

In 1957 Admiral Horthy lay dying in Estoril, where he had spent his own years in exile following the Russian invasion of Hungary. His conscience was still troubled. 'I, an old soldier, have broken my oath.' Responding to several pleas, Otto at last visited his villa. From his deathbed Horthy begged for political absolution, for having deprived him of his throne.

Today, his Imperial Highness Archduke Otto – or Dr Habsburg, as he prefers to be called – is a Euro MP for a German seat. He has adjusted to his altered status better than anyone else, and is the only royal to have run for elective office. His palace is not the Schönbrunn in Vienna, but the Palais de l'Europe in Strasbourg, the seat of the European Parliament. From it he is working to build a united Europe. His conception, he insists, is not, as it appears, to rebuild the Habsburg Empire of his father and Charles V.

Nevertheless, he has not forgotten who he is. Recently, in the corridors of Strasbourg, on the eve of a football international, Otto was asked if he intended to watch the Austria-Hungary match. He gazed intently at his colleague through thick spectacles. 'Who are they playing?'

Had Archduke Franz Ferdinand's chauffeur obeyed instructions on 28 June 1914, he would have continued driving along Appel Quay in Sarajevo. Instead he turned right down Franz Josef Strasse where the car passed close to a young student. The bullets fired by Gavrilo Princep that morning felled the first in a line of royal dominoes and led to the collapse of the Russian, the German and the Austro-Hungarian Empires.

The assassination in his territory of the heir presumptive to his throne prompted the Habsburg Emperor, Franz Josef, to subjugate the independent state responsible for sponsoring Princep. He sent his troops into Serbia. Tsar Nicholas II of Russia immediately came to Serbia's help. Emperor William of Germany responded by rushing to Franz Josef's side, whereupon George V of Britain, together with the French, jumped to the assistance of Russia. In the space of a month the essential unit of monarchy, that of the family, had disintegrated. Royal cousins were at war with each other. Few would survive as sovereigns. By 1918 most European kings and queens were jacks.

In 1914 Franz Josef 's family were not in much shape anyway. His wife, the beautiful Empress Elisabeth, had been stabbed to death on the shores of Lake Leman. His son Rudolph, along with his mistress, had committed suicide in a Mayerling shooting-lodge. (One story had it that he had been castrated by a jealous gamekeeper, and had killed himself in despair; another, more recent one, that he was murdered.) His brother, Maximilian, had been shot by a firing squad after proclaiming himself Emperor of Mexico. (Maximilian's wife, the Empress Charlotte, died after fifty years of insanity, still believing she was in her tropical palace.) His other brother Charles, a religious fanatic, had drunk the sacred waters in Jordan only to find that they were contaminated. He died soon after of typhoid.

One of his nephews, Charles's son Franz Ferdinand, was murdered at Sarajevo with his wife, while another, Charles's son Otto, led such a high life in Vienna that he died of venereal disease.

In a sense, the fortunes of his family were reflected in the rocky state of Franz Josef 's Empire – 'that worm-eaten galleon', as Bismarck called it. Each of the eleven or so nations which made up this Empire wanted greater independence from the Dual Monarchy of Austria and Hungary. The First World War was to give them just that; at a price.

On 21 November 1916 Franz Josef drank a cup of tea and died after a reign of sixty-eight years. His successor, his great-nephew Charles, was to reign for only two. Few careers have been more tragic.

One of Dr Habsburg's earliest memories is of his father's coronation in Budapest on a dull grey day in 1916. He was four years old, and in a white satin doublet with his gold locks looked for all the world like a Little Lord Fauntleroy. After watching Charles put on the Holy Crown of St Stephen, Otto was taken back through the slippery streets to the castle. From behind a window he saw the new Emperor on his rearing grey stallion swing his sword to all four corners of the compass. He would, he swore, defend his land from every quarter. It was to be no more than a noble gesture.

At twenty-nine, Charles had fought on the Russian front and in South Tyrol, but had never been trained for office. A pacifist in time of war, he was, like Yeats's Irish airman, allied to people he mistrusted and in battle against those he wished to befriend. For all his bravery and honesty, he lacked the guile required of a politician and the charisma needed for a leader. While his wife, the forceful Empress Zita, wrote to the Kaiser begging him not to bomb Rheims Cathedral, Charles tried to do 'all in my power to end as soon as may be the horror and sacrifice of the war'. Without any German sanction, his efforts for peace came to nothing. By the autumn of 1918 his Empire had been dismembered. Early in November, at Vienna's Schönbrunn Palace, Charles signed a manifesto in which he relinquished all participation in the affairs of state. He was only voluntarily abandoning power, he stressed. He was not abdicating. 'This crown is a responsibility given to me by God and I cannot renounce it.' His Naval Commander, Admiral Horthy, raised his right hand as the tears streamed down his face. 'I will never rest,' he pledged, 'till I have restored Your Majesty to his thrones in Vienna and Budapest.'

Charles and his family left Vienna shortly after. 'Herr Habsburg,' one government official is alleged to have said, 'your taxi is waiting.' Crammed in the back of a car, they drove to the shooting-lodge of Eckartsau in the damp meadows close to the Hungarian border. Next day Austria was proclaimed a republic. A few months later, the Habsburgs were forced into exile.

On 23 March 1919 Colonel Edward Strutt, a mountaineer and officer of the Royal Scots, led Charles, Zita and their children on to the train at Kopfstetten for the journey to Switzerland. A crowd of two thousand people, all silent, were there to see them off. Many were weeping. Seven hundred years ago,' said Charles, turning to Strutt, 'Rudolph of Habsburg came from Switzerland to Austria. Now I return to the starting point. After seven hundred years, Colonel, after seven hundred years.'

'My family has been exiled from France, Italy and Portugal,' Zita told Strutt over dinner. 'When I married I became an Austrian subject and now am an exile from Austria. Colonel Strutt, tell me, to what country do I now belong?' He could find no answer.

Once settled in his villa on Lake Geneva, Charles began plotting his return. 'I went into retirement . . . pending the restoration of order,' he insisted. 'I am still Emperor.' And in Budapest, the site of his coronation, he was officially just that. (What was more, loyal Admiral Horthy had dried his tears and returned to Hungary as Regent in Charles's absence.) Before long he had drummed up the support of the French Prime Minister, who promised in a seven-point verbal pact that if his restoration bid succeeded, France would immediately recognize him.

On 24 March 1921 Charles slipped out of Switzerland and caught a train to Vienna. Disguised as a Spanish diplomat called Sanchez, he wore, yes, a pair of dark glasses and pretended to be ill. By the time he crossed into Hungary, he had perked up considerably, having changed his glasses to large goggles and his name to William Codo, an official of the English Red Cross. The tension was becoming unbearable. At the first stop he was unable to finish a meal of gherkins – the remains of which were kept as a souvenir by the landlord. At the second, no one realized who the goggled man was but all drained their glasses in a toast to the King; everyone, that is, except Charles who found the wine too heavy. At last he drew up at his palace in Budapest. Quickly changing into uniform, he set off to find Horthy, to thank him for all his troubles, and to relieve him of the cares of state.

There are two versions of what happened next, but both agree that Charles was pleased to see the Regent. Horthy, on the other hand, was horrified to see his master. 'I assured His Majesty that were I able to recall him, our Crowned King whose legitimate interests I recognized and was prepared to defend, it would be the happiest moment of my present office.' (By implication the next twenty years must have been agonizing.) Now, alas, was not the time. 'The very moment I hand the reins of state over to the King, the armies of the neighbouring states will cross our frontiers.'

Charles then told him of the support promised by the French Prime Minister Briand. 'Should Briand accept the responsibility, I shall gladly restore your hereditary rights to Your Majesty.' Should he not, Charles would have to leave the country before his presence became known. Before telephoning France, he was hastily invested with the Military Order of Maria Teresa and created Duke of Otranto. (He claimed he never wore the Cross nor ever used the title.) Then he rang Briand. 'The answer was a definite denial.'

In Charles's account, Horthy emerges as man who has come to identify his country's interests rather too closely with his own. 'This is a disaster,' the Regent fumed, disentangling himself from the King's embrace. 'Your Majesty must leave at once and must return immediately to Switzerland.' Charles then explained the reasons for his visit. 'But what does Your Majesty offer me in return?' asked the exasperated Horthy; whereupon Charles gave him the title of Duke and a position as head of the armed forces. Horthy hedged. There was another thing: his oath to parliament on becoming Regent. 'But,' exploded Charles, 'before that you swore an oath to me.' When told of Briand's endorsement, Horthy finally backed down. Could he, though, have just one more decoration, the Grand Cross of the Order of Maria Teresa?

It was Briand's inevitable disclaimer which put an end to this first venture. He had wanted a *fait accompli* or nothing. Keen as he was to have a monarchist bulwark against Russia, he could not be seen to contravene Britain's 'categorical opposition' to a restoration. So Charles returned to Switzerland, where he found his hosts a little upset by this adventure. From then on he had to give two days' notice if he wanted to leave, and he was closely watched. 'They won't even let Otto sail his paper boats out there on the lake.'

Meanwhile, Horthy tried to smooth things out with a letter which he hoped would keep Charles away once and for all. The chances of a restoration were not particularly good at the moment, he wrote, but rest assured, 'I yearn impatiently for the moment when I can step down from this seat of tribulation.' He added a PS, not to forget that Grand Cross. The letter did not do the trick.

That autumn, as Mr and Mrs Kowno, Charles and Zita flew to western Hungary where some loyalist troops were waiting to advance by train on Budapest. Unfortunately, they landed a day early to find the train being used by peasants for transporting sugar-beet. There was a 24-hour hold-up while the trucks were unloaded and assembled. The delay was to prove fatal. When at last they set steam for Budapest, the admirable Horthy knew all about it. He gave orders to tear up the tracks and went around telling everyone that the Czechs were coming. After a rudimentary skirmish in the suburbs, Charles ordered a white flannel towel to be hoisted on the funnel. Leaning out of a carriage, he told his soldiers to cease fire. He had lost the stomach for a fight.

Still protesting that Horthy's measures were illegal, Charles and Zita were escorted on to a British ship in the Danube. 'A broken man and much more than a broken man is borne from Hungary on that funereal barque,' said one man who watched them leave. Having heard that the Swiss would have nothing more to do with him, Charles set sail for Madeira.

Though the Allies had agreed in principle to give Charles £20,000 a year, not a penny was forthcoming. Unlike his fellow monarchs, he had made no provision for exile. In fact, apart from his family jewels in Switzerland, the man who had once ruled over most of Europe had no funds at all. Unable to go on living in the Palace Hotel, he accepted the offer of a villa above Funchal. Like King Umberto's first residence in Sintra, the Quinta do Monte was lost in banks of fog. It had no electric light and one lavatory. Linen and crockery were supplied by the hotel. 'The poor Emperor has only vegetables and pudding for dinner,' wrote a lady-in-waiting. 'They have to economize so much that the Empress cannot even buy butter.' While Charles looked longingly at the ships sailing for Europe, his wife returned to Geneva to collect her children – the 'fallen Arches' as the press dubbed them – and the jewels. The Austrian lawyer in Zürich, in whose care they had been placed, proved to be as untrustworthy as Horthy. He had vanished, not unnaturally, with his charge. Some months later a member of the family traced him to Frankfurt, where he was living suspiciously under a different name. In language reminiscent of the Regent he said how delighted he was to get such a burden off his back. The jewels were safe in the bank and would be returned on the following day. He never turned up.

In March 1922 Charles went to buy a birthday present for one of his children. He did not take a coat and caught a cold. A few days later he retired to bed with a severe cough. It developed into pneumonia. Zita sold the last of her lace and jewellery to pay for medical supplies. Soon her husband was requiring oxygen. There were only two cylinders on the island and they were too heavy to bring to the villa. A number of toy balloons were filled, but the oxygen leaked out on the journey uphill. With it passed the life of the last Habsburg. According to Anatole France, he was the only honest man to emerge from the war, 'but he was a saint and nobody listened to him.' He may one day be recognized as such. The Cause of his Canonization was opened in 1949. All he needs is to be attributed with a miracle.

There is a quaint story concerning Otto's grandfather, the venereal Archduke Otto, who when on a bicycle tour came across a band of gipsies. An old crone asked to read his palm. 'I see death and disaster in all your family,' she muttered with not a little accuracy, 'but all will be retrieved in the future by one who will bear the same name as yourself.'

Zita had seen her son live through a childhood that has been described as pathological. After her husband's death, she did all she could to make him capable of fulfilling the gipsy's prophecy. Moving from Madeira to the Spanish fishing village of Lequeitio, Zita set about the task of training Otto as a future Emperor. An education committee of former ministers was established to give him rigorous tuition in all the languages of the Empire. Soon he had mastered Croatian, Czech and Spanish, besides German and Hungarian. At night, with the cretonne curtains drawn shut – Alfonso XIII called this the draughtiest house in Spain – Otto and Zita would read political memoirs and discuss newspaper leaders.

After a year in a monk's cell at Clairveaux, he moved with his family to Belgium. Together with the Count of Paris, he enrolled at the University of Louvain to read political and social sciences. 'Even if he were not an Emperor,' said a fellow student, 'he would still stand out as the university's first scholar.' There was no time for frivolity. In his spare time, he set himself tasks such as working out how the average working-class family spent its income. (His own family's income needed equally careful

scrutiny, relying as it did on donations from friends and supporters.)
Receiving a degree with 'la plus grande distinction', Otto went on to
complete a doctorate – written in German and translated by him into
French. If the Emperor Charles had been lacking in various disciplines,
Zita made certain no such charge could be laid against her son. In his soft
hat and immaculately pleated trousers, with the beginning of a dark
moustache on his lip – a lip that did not protrude in the manner of his
ancestors – Otto was probably the Habsburg most fully equipped for
office. The trouble was getting it.

With Horthy keeping him at arm's length, Hungary was out of the
question. After Charles's fiasco, anti-Habsburg feeling ran so high that
there was even a movement to have Lord Rothermere crowned King in
the wake of some interest he had shown in land reform. In the pages of
the *Daily Mail* he politely declined the offer. He possibly recalled his
experience of helping King Carol.

Austria seemed more likely. In December 1931 the Tyrol village of
Ampass declared Otto an honorary citizen. He was deeply moved. It was
the incentive he required to dedicate his life to returning home. In the
following year eighty-five communities followed Ampass's example. By
1938, a third of Austria had made Otto their honorary citizen.

In the winter of 1932 Otto was doing some work on his thesis in Berlin
when he was approached by Prince August Wilhelm, the Kaiser's son and
a Nazi. Would he consent to meeting Goering for dinner? Otto had no
objection, but then he learned that Hitler was to be present and would be
delighted to meet him. Otto left Berlin.

As Otto's support in Austria grew more fervent, it became clear that
Hitler saw the Habsburgs as an obstacle to his plan for bringing Vienna
into the Reich. Indeed, the slogan used to prevent him was 'Against
Hitler only a Habsburg'. On 24 July 1934 the Austrian Chancellor
Dollfuss agreed to meet Otto's representatives and discuss the possibility
of restoration. Next day a group of Nazis seized the Chancellery and
tried, unsuccessfully, to establish a Nazi government. In the scuffle,
Dollfuss was murdered. Otto immediately wrote to his successor
Schuschnigg, telling him it was the right moment for him to return. 'At
that time,' he says today, 'it looked very, very probable.' Schuschnigg
replied in the negative. He thought more time was needed. For some
minutes after receiving this news, Otto struggled to regain his self-
control. By his paleness, his sister could see how much he was moved.

Four years later, on hearing of Hitler's plan to invade, and at the instigation of Zita, Otto wrote again. 'From my standpoint as Austria's rightful Emperor, as legitimate heir to a dynasty that protected Austria for 650 years . . . as the son of my father . . . who sacrificed his life for his people to live on a far-off island, I cannot and will not be unfaithful to the task I have inherited . . . I urge you to turn over to me the Chancellorship.'

Addressing him as Your Majesty, Schuschnigg's reply was the same as before. Even if Austria had to capitulate, he wrote, it was better to do so without endangering the dynasty. After the war, Europe would reorganize itself and matters would be sorted out then.

Otto claimed afterwards that he could have stopped the Anschluss had he gone back. He was given no chance. On 11 March Hitler marched into Austria. Among the German staff, the code-name for the operation was 'Der Fall Otto' – the Otto case. As further proof of how much they feared this Habsburg's return, a price was put on his head. He was declared a traitor.

When war broke out, Otto flew to America to attempt to persuade Roosevelt that Austria had to be seen as a separate country and to press for its independence. In the Senate he was received as a ruling head of state. For the first time in twenty years, the senators all rose to their feet. In May 1940, smoking sixty cigarettes a day, Otto returned to Belgium and collected his family. An hour or two after they had left their home, on their way to Lisbon, a solitary German plane flew over it and dropped a bomb.

Settled safely in America, Otto's only war effort was the formation of an Austrian battalion in Indiana. It was a rather pathetic attempt to form the basis of a government in exile. It lasted three months and never moved from Camp Atterbury. Meanwhile the threat to his country was changing from Nazi to Communist. In 1944 he made a more substantial contribution by persuading Churchill and Roosevelt to divide Austria into four rather than two. This meant that Russia's influence was halved. 'Churchill was a great help. He was always very interested in establishing Austrian independence.' In fact, on the occasion of Otto's wedding in 1951, Churchill sent him a history of the Marlborough family bound in red morocco. The title-page was embossed with the Austrian crown and an inscription deplored the disintegration of Europe since the demolition of the Austro-Hungarian Empire.

The war had clearly put paid to any hopes of reconstituting this empire in its old form. From 1945 on Otto devoted himself to finding a new way of implementing the ideals of his ancestors. He travelled widely, he went on lecture tours to America, and in the German town of Pöcking (in a house known by wags as Pöckingham Palace) he set out his political ideas on paper. He spent ten years completing a biography of Charles V, whose ambition had been an *Orbis Europeanus christianus*, and wrote more than a dozen books to show how this ambition could be realized today.

It could be achieved, he thought, by taking a realistic look at what monarchy had to offer in the future, rather than what it had offered in the past. In an address to the Cambridge Royalist Party in 1960, entitled 'Monarchy in the Atomic Age', he urged his light blue audience to think of the monarchist idea as a political doctrine. 'We have lived in a republican cycle which really dates back to the Renaissance . . . Its end came, as I believe, at the hour when the first atomic bomb was dropped on Hiroshima. Consequently we are now living at the beginning of a new cycle . . . A new form of mixed government will have to be found – in other words, a new concept of monarchy . . . Only monarchy is capable of guaranteeing individual freedom in an atmosphere of general and social equality of rights.

Otto's concern was not with the trappings of monarchy, nor even necessarily the hereditary aspect; he was more concerned to return to the origin of kingship – to the monarch as both head of state and Chief Justice of the Supreme Court. The main weakness of a republic was that it lacked this Court of last Appeal.

By 1961, Otto felt he could finally abdicate his claim to the Austrian throne without compromising his political doctrine. Besides, if he was going to fight for a United States of Europe, there was no sense in being exiled from his own heartland. It took seven years of legal battles before he was allowed back. In August 1966 he quietly crossed the border with two children in the back of his open Volkswagen. Since then he has become something of an institution. In a 1969 popularity poll, he was ranked fourth – behind Herbert von Karajan.

Otto is not yet an emperor, nor probably ever will be. More important to him at the moment is the fact, 'I am a European'. Since 1979 he has been an energetic member of the European Parliament. It has given him 'the chance of carrying out in practice what I have been speaking and writing about all my life.' In his small white office in Strasbourg, he has after sixty years found a secure and relevant base from which to work at the Habsburg policy of integrating many different nations into a single unit, of building a federation without frontiers. When that comes about, there would have to be a European flag. 'Now we do possess a European symbol which belongs to all nations equally. This is the Cross of the Holy Roman Empire . . . ' There would also have to be a head of state. 'The solution must be essentially "monarchical".'

One chill sunny morning I visited Dr Habsburg at the Palais de l'Europe. The meeting had to be arranged long in advance. His diary, I was told, was booked up months ahead with engagements to speak in Munich, Northumberland, Switzerland.

Making my way through some people who were protesting about seal culls, I joined the man who would be Emperor of Austria-Hungary in the canteen. He was a tall bird-like man in glasses with brown eyes that burned with missionary zeal. He came over more as a professor and diplomat than a leader of men, but he had a politician's fluency, and the ability to appear to answer questions when in fact leap-frogging them. He used his hands when he spoke and was keener to talk about 'a common organ for foreign policy' than himself. Over a cup of coffee, I asked innocently if he could recite his names and titles. 'Ah, Holy Moses, no. I have twenty-four first names and I don't know them all. As for the titles, which I've renounced' – except for his claim to the throne of Hungary – 'they make up the page of a book. I wouldn't be able to recite them either.' The name Habsburg, however, was a help. 'The past teaches you a lot of patience,' he answered in reply to a question about his hopes for monarchy. 'I am historian enough to know that you cannot exclude anything. In politics you should never say never.' He made a gesture with his hands. 'The main thing is we should advance.'

In advancing Dr Habsburg is not going to storm for the stars. 'If I have learnt something in my life, it's that if you try to make the first step before the second, you fall on your face, and I don't want to' – he corrected himself '—I don't want Europe to fall on its face.' The correction, I thought, said it all.

8

Dr Ferdinand

'But war's a game which were their subjects wise Kings would not play at.'

THE TASK, COWPER

On the afternoon of 10 November 1918, Count Godard Bentinck was sitting in his library at Amerongen in Holland, watching the rain come down. He had returned early to his castle from a shooting-party and was enjoying a cigar when the telephone rang. It was the Dutch Foreign Office. The Kaiser had just crossed the border. Would he take him in for three days? The count told them to ring back. When they did, three hours later, he explained he had neither coal nor petrol to heat the house. He was promised a truck-load of coal that same night and all the petrol he needed. There was no way now of refusing refuge to a man who, whatever else he might have been, was a fellow Knight of St John.

Earlier in the day, a car had driven out of the fog at a frontier post near Eijsden. A man had got out and seeing a Dutch soldier loitering had walked up to him and handed the astonished man his sword. 'I am the German Emperor,' he explained. While frantic messages were relayed to the capital, the Kaiser waited at the railway station. He waited for six hours, until his passage was cleared and his long black royal train was allowed across the border. Next day, at 3 o'clock in the afternoon, in a cold drizzle, it steamed into the small town of Maarn. The Count was there to greet him.

'Well,' said the Kaiser, climbing into a car. 'What do you think of this?' He said nothing more. He was, according to the Count, 'stunned beyond comprehension'.

In the failing light they crossed the canal into Amerongen.

'Now,' the Kaiser said, rubbing his hands, 'give me a cup of real good English tea.'

Whatever Emperor William II of Germany was thinking as he munched his flapjacks, it cannot have been pleasant. On that same day, 11 November, an armistice had been signed putting an end to a conflict which had resulted in the loss of some ten million lives and been branded in his name as The Kaiser's War. The most admired, most feared, most talked about man in the world, a man of histrionic talents and for thirty years a monarch by the Grace of God, was now in exile. As the All-Highest, he had once given to the congregation of a garrison church Bibles in which he wrote, 'I will walk among you and be your God and ye shall be my people.' What on earth, he must have wondered, was God doing now?

It was this delusion that he was an instrument of Providence which had prevented the Kaiser from abdicating. Had he done so a month before in favour of his grandson, the monarchy and the Hohenzollern dynasty might have been saved. He did not, and goaded by the Communists, his country had drifted towards civil war. President Wilson refused to make peace with a Hohenzollern and the Allies were determined to make Germany a republic. 'Nous leur fouterons la république,' said Clemenceau, not mincing his words. There was no way out for the government. Behind the Kaiser's back, the Chancellor had announced on 9 November that he had, in fact, abdicated and that his son, Crown Prince William, had renounced the succession. It was too late to prevent the revolution, and on the advice of his High Command, the Emperor was told to leave. 'I could not let the Kaiser be deposed by the mob,' the Chancellor explained. 'I had no other choice.'

In power, the Kaiser had once grumbled unconvincingly that people thought he was the Supreme Commander. 'They are greatly mistaken. The general staff tells me nothing and never asks my advice. I drink tea, go for walks and saw wood.' In the unofficial prison of Amerongen, where he was to spend not three days but seventeen months, this more or less summed up his régime. He rose early from his bed, a narrow four-poster in which another autocrat, Louis XIV, had slept. From his window he could watch the villagers skating on the moat, and over the trees, the masts of ships sailing up the Rhine to Germany, seventy miles away. In the morning, followed by a detective on a bicycle – there were some 140 guards in all – he sauntered in his serge suit and homburg hat to the nearby forest. For three hours every day the man who had just sawn off the branch on which he was sitting, spent his time in chopping wood. During the course of his stay at Amerongen, the Imperial lumberjack was to clear half an acre of several thousand small Scotch firs, and cut them neatly into stacks. After a good hack, he usually repaired to a summer-house where, over port and cigars, he would pore over maps and retrace his battles with a finger. He bitterly resented the premature announcement of his abdication, which he had actually signed a month later. It had made him seem as if he were running away. As usual he blamed everyone but himself. For a man whose nature was alien to self-criticism, it must have been difficult for him to comprehend the surge of demands to 'hang the Kaiser'. After an attempt by some American soldiers to kidnap him, his wife would wake up screaming, 'They are coming for him!' They never did. The Allies demanded his extradition, but the Dutch refused.

In common with most other monarchs, except the Tsar, the Kaiser's removal from his throne had been a bloodless operation. He was not strung up by his heels, the fate that befell dictators. If there were no moves afoot to make him a saint, like Emperor Charles of Austria, at least he was permitted to keep a large part of his fortune, which in exile amounted to 600 million gold marks. It enabled him, in the spring of 1920, to buy the house and sixty-acre estate of Doorn, seven miles from Amerongen. Here he settled down to the life of an English country gentleman. He even spoke like one. Phrases like 'a damn topping good fellow' rolled easily from his tongue. In his study, surrounded by busts of himself and the Queen's Cup he had won at Cowes, he sat on a saddle-stool and answered the letters which were carried to him in washing baskets. He went for walks in the village, touching his hat to everyone he met, and he set about felling trees again. A Court of sorts was kept to preserve appearances. Whenever he was invited out to dinner, a man would be sent in advance to see who would be there, what they would eat and where they would sit. Apart from introducing their daughters to him, the Dutch aristocracy showed no particular interest. Anyone who did was recommended Van Harten's café opposite. For twenty-five cents an hour, from the enormous top-floor balcony, the public could have a good look at what went on in the Emperor's house and garden.

It is not likely they would have got value for money. The old fire and verve had gone. His once proud moustache was no longer waxed. His hair was whitened, his eyes had paled and his complexion had gone the colour of putty. 'It was a grey man we gazed upon,' recalls one visitor. 'Grey of dress, of face, of hair and steely of eye.' One thing the Kaiser had not lost was his gift of the gab and his knack of approaching everything with an 'open mouth'. (In former days, a policeman had overheard a boy tell how his father thought the Kaiser was an old windbag. The man had been sent to prison.) At the morning service, held near the stairs, he read out sermons; and in the evenings, sipping hock, he read out erudite papers he had written on the origin and development of the palanquin or the history and meaning of the Chinese monad. Sometimes when reading P.G. Wodehouse aloud to his family he would laugh when there was no joke at all, to test the reactions of his audience. Then, after everyone had brushed the tears from their eyes, he would ask them to explain what was so funny.

The Kaiser's immediate family suffered perhaps more than he did. His wife Augusta died heartbroken in 1921, having spent her time knitting clothes for the poor children of Germany. His playboy son, Crown Prince William, was interned on the remote island of Wieringen in the Zuider Sea. There he vegetated 'under the most impossible of conditions' in a house without a bathroom. Pleas to his cousin George V went unheeded. He had never been very popular with the British. On a shooting-party in England, the guns were told by their host: 'Please don't shoot the Kaiser. His son is much worse yet.'

The only comfort the Kaiser found was in the arms of a stocky widow – whom he married in 1922 – and in the company of the Crown Prince's children, for whom in the words of his favourite grandson, Louis Ferdinand, 'Doorn became a second home.'

On his eleventh birthday, 11 November 1918, Louis Ferdinand was invited to Berlin's New Palace by his grandmother, the Kaiser's first wife. Just before tea-time she entered the drawing-room in tears with the announcement that the revolution had broken out and the war was lost. Louis Ferdinand's first reaction was one of relief. 'And why? Because I concluded that I would not have to attend the Military School at Plön.'

At that time he seemed an unlikely candidate one day to head the House of Hohenzollern and embody the hopes of German monarchists. Had the Kaiser abdicated when he was advised to, in October 1918, it would have been in favour of Louis Ferdinand's eldest brother, William, a soldier-crazed boy with whom he was always scrapping. One thing Louis Ferdinand hated was Prussian militarism as exemplified by both his brother and his tutor, for whom the infantry regulations and the state railway timetable were mankind's most perfect achievements. 'I had a profound dislike for any kind of authority and discipline,' he confessed, also acknowledging that he was the black sheep of the family. He was a rebel prince from an early age. At his birthplace in Potsdam – now a restaurant for Russian troops – he would walk back and forth past the sentry box in the park so that each time the guard would have to salute him. When, in common with many other royal children, an English governess was forced on him, he told the bewildered Miss Grimble that unless she went away, 'I shall call a forester and have you shot on the spot.' If anything he had inherited his mother's Russian blood. Once when asked by the Kaiserin if he liked being German, he had shocked her by saying he would rather be Russian. The only infringement made on him by the war was the news of the Tsar's assassination. 'I sat for a whole afternoon on a little hill all by myself musing about the horrible end of these relatives of ours.'

With the war over, in between trips to Doorn, with his mother, he passed from Potsdam High School into the University of Berlin. By this time, 'I had become a staunch republican, believing firmly in the advantages of the Weimar Republic.' With a wrist made supple from drinking bouts and duels, Louis Ferdinand took up the violin and forsook the duties of a Prussian prince for the pleasures of the opera house and concert hall. His first taste of freedom came with the offer of a trip to Argentina, which the Kaiser endorsed. 'He always supported my rather adventurous character.' The journey was to give him the idea for his thesis on immigration. Back in Germany, in a rented room on a stipend of £100 a month, he developed into an intellectual snob, a bookworm and, by his own admission, a sour puss. 'I was,' he said, 'extremely unsociable.'

All this changed in the spring of 1927. Fresh from a seminar on the categorical imperative of Immanuel Kant, he joined some friends for dinner in a Berlin restaurant. Among their number was the film star Lili Damita, born of Portuguese parents and brought up in France. For Louis Ferdinand, it was love at first sight. Under the spell of Lili's brown eyes, blonde hair and infectious smile, he came very quickly to her conclusion that there were other things in life besides intellectual ambition. He cut his hair, manicured his nails and took her to nightclubs, where he trod on her toes. She told him to take more physical exercise, so he played tennis, swam and boxed – with such energy that he had a heart attack. After two months in bed he extracted a fur coat and a two-seater sports car from his grandfather. 'If he goes on like that,' grumbled the Kaiser, 'I shall be broke before long.' The idea of marriage was beginning to take hold. 'I shall follow you to the end of the earth,' he promised Lili when she returned to Hollywood, but was careful not to do so until he had completed his studies. In 1929 his thesis was accepted *cum laude*. He became the first Hohenzollern to receive a Doctorate. As a reward the Kaiser gave him a trip to the United States. The real reason, which he kept secret, was to see Lili. After being given an introduction to Roosevelt, who lectured him for an hour on the American constitution, he hurried on to Los Angeles. 'I have come all the way from Berlin to meet you again,' he told her breathlessly on the phone.

They spent a day on the sand at Santa Monica which filled his eyes with such stars that he did not bother to question how a story in next day's paper could have been so accurate in every detail. (He was so high he even took up flying lessons.) 'Since we are in love,' she purred on another beach, 'why shouldn't we get married?' Tijuana was proposed for the ceremony, but meanwhile he had to earn some money. One of the people he had met on his way to Hollywood was the industrialist Henry Ford. Ford had offered him a job, so Louis Ferdinand turned up at the local branch and was hired as a labourer. Wearing locomotive overalls and, in the position where he would normally wear his order of the Black Eagle, a number 113 badge, he had become a proletarian. At the same time, a little sanity had returned in his relationship with Lili. He discovered that the Duke of Kent had enjoyed quite a time with her; also that Hollywood 'as far as publicity is concerned is one of the most dangerous places'. Alarmed by press reports of an imminent wedding, his family had sent him urgent orders to go south to Buenos Aires. 'I didn't react very favourably to these admonitions.' But then came another cable. ' "Dear Dr Ferdinand" – that was my official name at the Ford factory – "please go to Buenos Aires. You can come back whenever you want or when you have cooled down. And don't ever do anything against the wishes of your grandfather. Signed Henry Ford." ' The only person with whom he was to make the Tijuana trip was a friendly mechanic from the Ford factory.

So, at the instigation of his employer, Louis Ferdinand sailed for Argentina where he worked for a year on an assembly line in Calle Vallefane. After being arrested in his car without a licence ('We are not used,' the police said, 'to princes driving round in dirty overalls') he returned for a stint at the Ford plant in Detroit. 'Louis, my boy,' one fellow worker advised him, 'never forget this. If you keep your ass flat on the ground, you cannot fall very high.' It did not prove difficult to do. Dry America, with its bathtub gin, had converted him into a near alcoholic. (When Roosevelt ended prohibition, he sent a telegram of congratulations. It had to be substantially edited, because it 'smelled a bit too much of liquor'.) His greatest achievement was to sell Ford cars to the brewers. They were deadly enemies of the teetotal Ford, but Louis Ferdinand's state convinced them that the man could not be so bad if he had such representatives.

Before he left America to dry out in Doorn, Louis Ferdinand had another meeting with Lili. She had just come back from France and phoned to ask if he would meet her in Chicago. The story was in the newspapers before he even got there. At last he clicked as to how much of a publicity stunt he had been. As Geoffrey Bocca has observed, when a prince falls in love with a showgirl, it may be he who provides the car, but it is she who takes him for a ride. 'I wonder if Lili Damita ever loved me,' he wrote later with touching faith. 'I have never found out. But at least she did not destroy my illusion.'

In 1933 the democratic prince spent three months recuperating in the Kaiser's care. He sawed wood, he fed the ducks, and he helped his grandfather in the rose garden. 'I think it a damn shame that he never went to the States,' Louis Ferdinand regretted later with a touch of naïvety, 'because if he had, there certainly wouldn't have been a war, because the Americans would have adored him, and he the same way.' He was preparing to go back to America for good when news came of his brother's marriage to a commoner. The Kaiser was a firm believer in his family marrying people of equal birth. A good breeder did not mix thoroughbreds with Percherons. He was heartbroken. Over tea, an obviously dangerous meal for Hohenzollerns, he told his grandson that there was no question of him returning to Detroit. 'You'll have to take your brother's place and settle down in Germany.'

The Kaiser had good reason to be concerned. In 1933 hopes of a Hohenzollern restoration were higher than they had been for some time – and until then they had not been very bright. In 1925 an extraordinary book was published by a German secret agent known mysteriously as X.7. It was called *The Return of the Kings* and promised on its title-page to reveal the facts about a conspiracy for the restoration of monarchy in Central Europe.

Shortly after the war, X.7. was rapping his knuckles in retirement somewhere in the Alps. He wondered what to do next. Should he write his memoirs? No, he concluded. They 'would probably be so unconvincing in their revelations that no publisher would print them.' What the publisher did print was unconvincing enough. One autumn morning X.7. was disturbed in his reverie by a telegram bearing the ominous words: 'Shall be with you tomorrow afternoon. Albrecht.' This was a bolt from the blue. The man was head of the greatest secret service in Europe. Next day the bell rang, and Albrecht's familiar and exceedingly well-modulated voice delivered the news that 'we are again standing on the brink of a catastrophe.' X.7. was being hauled from his hideaway to prevent it. Slightly puzzled – and no wonder – he caught a train to Berlin where a Major von Keller told him what was happening. Apparently a Russian organization calling itself the Third Internationale had decided to make mischief and destroy not only order and liberty, but also Christianity throughout the world. 'Unfortunately for herself, as well as for the rest of Europe, Germany did not realize this world danger when she let Bolshevism loose upon Russia.' In 1917 the Germans had packed Lenin on a train and sent him into Russia 'like a plague bacillus', according to Churchill. The Communist contagion, however, had not confined itself to Russia – as the German revolution proved. The only cure, explained von Keller, was the re-establishment of monarchy in Central Europe. 'We must work towards the unification of German Royal Houses. When a Hohenzollern sits once more on the throne of Frederick the Great . . . when a Habsburg is again crowned King of Hungary at Budapest and a Romanoff returns to St Petersburg, then the world will no longer need to tremble because there will be some security restored to it.'

X.7.'s brief was to sound out various royals for their acquiescence in this conspiracy. He visited Empress Zita in Spain, who told him to go away; and he saw Louis Ferdinand's mother in Berlin, who believed the Hohenzollerns were still too unpopular to do more than wait for a change in public opinion. She would bring up her sons so that they would be ready when called upon, and no more. 'In a word, I hate intrigue.' And that was the end of X.7.'s mission.

The German government was to be a better bet than the secret service. In 1930 Chancellor Brüning thought of stemming Hitler's rise by bringing back the Hohenzollerns. The Socialists had no intention of dragging the Kaiser out of his woods. They were, though, prepared to support a regency in favour of Louis Ferdinand's brother. Not on, said President Hindenburg, showing belated loyalty to his old master; the Kaiser or nothing. (His political will, suppressed by Hitler, was to be more flexible. He wished for a restoration of the monarchy.)

In 1932 Goering visited Doorn and told the Kaiser of Hitler's desire to reinstate him. Meanwhile Hitler was telling Louis Ferdinand's father, a man he thought interested only in horses and women, that his goal was 'the restoration of the Empire under a Hohenzollern'. The Crown Prince was taken in, and with his brother tagged along behind the Nazis.

Even the Allies were beginning to regret what they had done. On a trip to England, Louis Ferdinand made a call on Lloyd George. After tea they went for a walk. 'You know, Prince Louis,' said the Welshman, sitting on a bench, 'we over here never expected nor intended the fall of your dynasty. In the face of public opinion in Britain at that time, it would have been impossible for me as Prime Minister to conclude a peace with either your grandfather or your father. But we all thought that a regency for your brother William would be set up under your mother and one of your uncles. If your family had remained in power in Germany, I am certain that Mr Hitler would not be giving us any headaches right now.'

If he accepted his position as head of the family, Louis Ferdinand was prevented from doing anything with it in the knowledge that his grand-father, his father and his elder brother were still alive. Nor did Hitler, once he had become Chancellor, encourage him. On the one occasion they met, Hitler delivered a forty-minute monologue on his admiration for Herr Ford. It rose to a high pitch as he proclaimed a wish for all Germans to have motor cars so that they would not have to walk. Ironically, it was Louis Ferdinand's American outlook that was to be the fly in the ointment. Following a period at Lufthansa, he joined the Luftwaffe where he was accused of undermining discipline at the base. His terrible crime was to eat in the canteen and associate with privates. His attitude was 'altogether too democratic' for the military men who might have supported his claim. This crime was soon compounded by another. In 1938 after his marriage to Grand Duchess Kira – the daughter of the Russian Pretender – Louis Ferdinand embarked on a long honeymoon, in the course of which he met Roosevelt again. The American President, who by now had become 'almost a second father' to him, entrusted the Prince with a delicate task. He was to sound out von Ribbentrop on the possibility of a meeting between Roosevelt, Mussolini, Hitler and Chamberlain. On returning to Germany Louis Ferdinand duly sent a memorandum to the Foreign

Minister. It was met with a stony silence. That Christmas he cabled Roosevelt thanking him for his hospitality. The message had hardly gone off when a man appeared at his house. He had been sent by Hitler. He wanted to know how Louis Ferdinand dared to communicate with Germany's greatest enemy.

In 1940 Louis Ferdinand's brother was killed on a French battlefield. Some 50,000 people walked past his coffin at Potsdam. It was a show of monarchist sympathy that infuriated Hitler into withdrawing every Hohenzollern prince from the armed forces. They were not to be made into martyrs. Louis Ferdinand, who had been a night-flight instructor – 'fortunately, I didn't have to throw bombs on anyone' – retired to supervise his grandfather's estate at Cadinen in East Prussia. He kept a low profile and took up playing the organ. In June 1941 came news that the Kaiser had a clot of blood in his lung. Louis Ferdinand rushed to his bed. His death on 3 June went unnoticed by the world. He had died, according to a Movietone announcer, eighty-two years too late. His body, in compliance with his will, was not taken back to Germany; he was buried under his favourite rhododendron bush.

If Louis Ferdinand's position became less cramped as a result, he was still conscious of his father's existence. It was this which probably made his involvement with the German Resistance so ineffectual. He had been approached by them as early as 1939. 'They hoped with my connections in the US, and especially with Roosevelt, I could be of some help.' His experience on the shop floor, they thought, would make him acceptable to the work-force. 'Their main aim was to stop the war and we knew they could only stop this war by getting rid of Hitler. After a while they would have put me on the throne.'

He threw musical soirées in his Berlin home so that the collaborators could meet. After the invasion of Russia in 1941, he even called on a prominent German general. 'I told him I thought it was high time that the army acted against Hitler and that I was ready to issue an order because of my right to the throne.' The general told him to keep quiet. So, more emphatically, did his father. There was nothing for it but to return to his organ.

In July 1944 Hitler narrowly escaped an assassination attempt. All but two of those involved – all Louis Ferdinand's friends were caught, and hanged by piano wire from butcher's hooks.

Louis Ferdinand had no idea whom they had implicated before dying.

At the beginning of August, he went to buy some tickets at his local railway station. In the light of the Russian advance, he had thought it prudent to evacuate his family. On returning to Cadinen through a torrent of rain, he was informed that two gentlemen from the Gestapo had been waiting since noon. Would it take long, he asked them. 'That depends.' Requesting them to wait a little longer, he changed into dry clothes, and took his wife into the study. 'I said one thing we've got to do, we've got to hide Roosevelt's picture which was on my writing-desk.' It was signed to him 'from your very dear friend'. 'So she took it, doubled it up and put it in her dress.' Placing some glasses, a bottle of Marsala and several cigars on the desk he rang for the two men. They appeared with a woman carrying a typewriter. Sitting the three of them down opposite a portrait of the Kaiser, Louis Ferdinand asked ingenuously what gave him the honour of their visit. 'Well, they said, we would like to know what you have been doing these last few months.' Believing that truth was always the best lie, he told them. He had attended one university lecture and otherwise spent his time shooting and drinking. 'They never asked me about my friends, fortunately.' The interview lasted seven hours, during which time he poured out the wine. 'We all got pretty gay and tight' – so much so that he helped compose the harmless report. Light with relief at not being given away, he was even set to type it out.

In January 1945 Russian troops were closing in on Cadinen. Louis Ferdinand's family had already departed for Potsdam. He remained to the end, and then in the bitter cold crossed the frozen river Haff on a sledge. It was the last time he saw his estate. Half an hour later, the Russians reached the river.

Louis Ferdinand had survived the war in buoyant spirits compared with his father. Racked with nicotine poisoning, Crown Prince William was a broken man. Twice he had seen his country disintegrate; he had lost two sons and his house at Potsdam. His only consolation was a hairdresser and chambermaid called Stefi Ritl with whom he spent the last years of his life. He died in 1951 in a dirty little house in Hechingen, looking out at Hohenzollern castle from where his forefathers had ridden out one fine day 700 years before.

Today Louis Ferdinand lives in a modern bungalow in a Berlin suburb, in a street appropriately called King's Way. He is the most human of the pretenders; a warm man with a ruddy face, a pointed nose and the kindly disposition of a golden retriever. Since 1951 he has had the air of someone who has lost the scent. In America, he was once asked what his business was. 'I'm in the pretender business!' he replied. Did it pay well? He didn't know – yet. His position as head of the House of Hohenzollern has brought him few perks so far – much less than his position as the German representative of Ford's from which he retired ten years ago. (He was once reproached, by the wife of a famous artist, for his horrible mid-western slang. 'Why don't you talk like your father?' she badgered. 'You see, Madam,' he replied, 'my father speaks with an Oxford accent, I prefer the Ford accent.') He gets VIP treatment when buying theatre tickets, but that is all. Like Otto he is a believer in a united Europe – the modern equivalent of an empire. Like Otto, 'I always say nothing is impossible in politics.' He believes that German people like to be led, and that bearing in mind their mentality monarchy is still the best thing for them. If he had been on the throne, he is 'pretty certain that Hitler would never have risen to power. And there wouldn't have been a holocaust or anything.' It may not be too late, though. He remains encouraged by the odd show of public support. At a recital in Berlin's Tatiana theatre he was once cheered by the audience with shouts of 'Long live the Emperor!' In 1968 a newspaper conducted an opinion poll for the next president. Louis Ferdinand topped it with 55 per cent. 'I don't believe even the newspaper which started the poll believed the reaction would be so favourable.' Unlike his grandfather, he does not see himself as a bailiff of God. 'I accept the present and try to make the best of it, but I would like to keep the door open for the future.' The future is in the hands of a seven-year-old grandson – his two eldest sons having renounced their rights by marrying commoners. He will still need the help of the Almighty. But 'with God's help and if the German people want it' the boy will be ready.

9

Imperial Mist

'There is very little indeed in the practice of the modern republican rulers which could be considered an improvement on the system by the Tsars, the Kaisers and the Caesars of the Holy Roman Empire.'

ALEXANDER, GRAND DUKE OF RUSSIA

In the spring of 1917 the Germans put Lenin into a sealed truck and sent him to the Baltic. From there he went to Petrograd, where they hoped he would foment a revolution, enabling them to defeat Russia. Only God knew what might happen. Three weeks later he put in an appearance. He was plainly worried at the prospect of a system which would show there was nothing sacred about his kings.

On 13 May 1917 three young Portuguese children were watching their flocks in the meadows of Cova de Iria – a place now better known as Fatima. Suddenly they heard a noise 'like a horse-fly in an empty water pot' and saw, on top of a small evergreen about two feet high, a ball of light. In its centre stood a woman. She was from Heaven, she told them, and if they returned at the same time for the next six months she would say what she wanted. She was true to her word. On her third appearance, on 13 July 1917, before a crowd of about three thousand people, she once more addressed the children. 'I come to ask the consecration of Russia to my immaculate heart.' If this was done, she would convert Russia and there would be peace. If not, 'the errors of Russia will spread through every country in the world.' No such conversion took place. Today, the former monarchies of Russia, East Germany, Hungary, Czechoslovakia, Albania, Bulgaria, Romania, Poland, Yugoslavia and Afghanistan are under Communist rule.

103

Inevitably, the Russian Empire was the first to go. The following July, shortly before midnight, in the mining town of Ekaterinburg, Tsar Nicholas and his family were woken up and ordered to come downstairs. Citizen Romanoff, as he was known by the drunken pilfering guards, dressed, put on a military cap and carried his son downstairs. In the trail of her 'poor, weak-willed hubby' came the Empress Alexandra, their four daughters and three retainers. They filed past the bathroom – from which the door had been removed – and the piano room where Olga and Tatiana had been forced to play songs like 'Let's Forget the Old Régime'. Assembling downstairs in a small wooden-floored room with a vaulted ceiling, they were instructed to wait for transport to arrive. Three chairs were brought in. Then a man entered, flanked by eleven guards and read out an order. The Tsar did not understand. 'What?' he asked. He was shot rising from his chair. The rest of the family and their retainers were murdered where they stood.

That night the bodies were wrapped in sheets and carried to a forest several miles away. Over the course of the next three days they were dismembered, burnt and dissolved in sulphuric acid. The macabre remains were thrown down an abandoned mine-shaft.

When the White Russians took Ekaterinburg soon after, they hurried to the two-storeyed house. In the downstairs room, which had been scrubbed clean, they discovered twenty-seven bullet-holes, some pornographic cartoons of the Empress and Rasputin, and upside-down at knee-height a message scribbled on the wall in German: *'Betsatzar ward in selbigen nacht/ Von Seinen Knechten umgebracht'* – 'On the same night **Belsatzar [sic] was killed by his slaves.'** In another room, howling, they found the spaniel called Joy which had belonged to the haemophiliac Alexei.

All that remained in the mine-shaft were some clothes, a finger, fourteen false teeth, and the corpse of Tatiana's lap-dog Jemmy. Eleven bodies were destroyed on the night of 16 July 1918. Jemmy's was the only one to survive.

Nicholas II had struck Queen Marie of Romania as someone who inhabited 'a sort of imperial mist'. He certainly died as he had lived. There are several versions of what happened that night, in most of which the lunatic element embraces rather more than a fringe. One account, *The File on the Tsar* by T. Mangold and A. Summers, is somewhat less fanciful. In summarizing it, one must go back two years. Recent evidence has shown

The Kaiser feeding instructions to his generals before the outbreak of war in 1914

The Kaiser feeding his ducks in exile at Doorn, Holland, after the war

The Kaiser's grandson and heir, Prince Louis Ferdinand Hohenzollern. 'Looking back, I believe that the popularity of our dynasty could have been much greater had we someone like the modern American public relations expert.'

*Princes of the Blood were ever falling for Hollywood queens. Louis Ferdinand paid court to
the actress Lili Damita. She spurned him for Errol Flynn*

Left: The Grand Duchess Anastasia, thought to have been stabbed to death in 1918. *Right:* 'Anna Anderson', who surfaced in a Berlin canal in 1920 claiming to be Anastasia and to have survived the massacre

The Tsar and his family on a conservatory roof in Tobolsk, where they were interned until April 1918

Top left: Orélie-Antoine de Tounens, the first King of Araucania and Patagonia
Above: Prince Philippe d'Araucanie, heir to his kingdom
Left: Sir James Brooke, the first white Rajah of Sarawak

King Zog of Albania in a national dress, flanked by his mother and sisters

Leka I, son of Zog, with his wife, Susan, and mother, Queen Geraldine, in 1975. A genuine soldier-king, he runs a paramilitary outfit with the aim of freeing Albania

Crown Prince Alexander of Yugoslavia with his father, King Peter, in 1955. The last time Alexander saw his country was in a Claridges suite. It was declared Yugoslav soil for the occasion of his birth

A family outing to Jerez. Dom Pedro of Brazil is second from left. Princess Elisabeth of Yugoslavia is in the middle talking to her cousin, Alexander, and his wife

The great white hope. Juan Carlos of Spain, restored to his throne in 1975, at the christening near Seville of Alexander's twins. Born to rule – they have the blood of most royal families in their veins – they seem destined to become anything but kings

that in 1916 the Kaiser was keen to sue for a separate peace with Russia. With his consent, the German brother of the Empress Alexandra, Grand Duke Ernst Ludwig of Hesse, went to St Petersburg under the pseudonym of Thurn-und Taxis. His proposals were rebuffed by the Tsar.

In the following spring, after abdicating from his railway carriage, Nicholas was interned with his family and accused of having plotted with the Germans. George V, his look-alike cousin, reneged on an offer of asylum because their presence in Britain might compromise his own position. The Kaiser, who was similarly related to the Tsar, and more closely to his wife, decided to rescue the Romanoffs. His decision was prompted not only by humanitarian feelings, but also by a desire to restore the monarchy in Russia with a puppet tsar – more accurately a regent. The man he had in mind was Grand Duke Ernst Ludwig of Hesse. He warned Kerensky, the head of the provisional government, that if one hair of the family's head were harmed, 'I would hold him personally responsible.' He still had to contend with Nicholas's refusal to seek sanctuary 'at any price' in a country with whom his own was still at war. With Lenin's rise to power the situation became more urgent. Lenin's need to win time for consolidating Bolshevism resulted in the spring of 1918 with the Treaty of Brest-Litovsk, a peace with the Germans which 'passed all understanding'. With the Bolsheviks at their mercy, the Germans were given vast chunks of Russian territory. It is also known that they made overtures on behalf of the Romanoffs.

A combination of Nicholas's reluctance to leave and Lenin's use of him as a pawn to keep the Germans at a safe distance, meant that nothing happened. The Kaiser, who spent 'sleepless nights in mourning over the Romanoffs' fate', decided to kidnap them. Although, as the events of 16 July bear out, the plan went horribly wrong, it was not the end of the story. The only person to die that day, in a military execution, not a room, was Tsar Nicholas II – and possibly his son.

There is evidence, albeit circumstantial, to suggest that the Empress and her daughters may not have been massacred in Ekaterinburg. Throughout the autumn of 1918 the Germans, who had an impressive intelligence service, as well as a mission in the mining town, continued to bargain for the 'Tsarina and children'. The founder of the Soviet secret police admitted that the women had not been killed that night. Another high-ranking Communist, Grigory Zinoviev, let slip that they were living 'in a city in Siberia'. In September, the Empress's sister, the Marchioness of Milford Haven, received news from her brother the Grand Duke that 'he had heard from two trustworthy sources that Alix [Alexandra] and all the children are alive.'

'On 17 July,' according to the British High Commissioner, Sir Charles Eliot, 'a train with the blinds down left Ekaterinburg for an unknown destination and it is believed that the surviving members of the Imperial Family were in it.' Clues point to the town of Perm, 200 miles to the north-west, as its destination. The eyewitness account of a nurse testifies to the fact that her brother was a guard at a house in Obvinskaya Street where 'the former Imperial Family were kept very secretly.' Satisfying her curiosity he led her to a basement room where by the light of a tallow candle 'I could make out the former Empress Alexandra Feodorovna and her four daughters who were in a terrible state.' Eighteen witnesses testified to an escape made by one of the daughters on 21 September. At midday, a girl in a white blouse was caught in the woods by some Red Army troops. After being beaten up she was escorted back to Perm with a swollen nose. At five in the evening a doctor was called to her side. 'I asked her "Who are you?" In a trembling voice, but quite distinctly, she answered me . . . "I am the daughter of the ruler, Anastasia." ' Following her escape the family were moved to a local convent, but for three days after, a company of Red Army men continued to search the woods. They never found the person they were looking for.

At the same time, Count Carl Bonde, a Swedish Red Cross delegate was making a journey by rail through the area. At one point 'the train was stopped and searched in order to find the Grand Duchess Anastasia, daughter of Tsar Nicholas II. The Grand Duchess was, however, not aboard the train. Nobody knew where she had gone.' Anastasia had obviously escaped again.

The trail of the others peters out soon afterwards. Another witness refers to the Empress and her three daughters being moved on to the town of Glozov. By this time they had become redundant as hostages. With Germany's defeat, the Bolsheviks could exterminate whom they wanted – as was proved by the execution of four Grand Dukes in January 1919.

The majority of Romanoffs to escape were those interned at an estate in the Crimea. They included Nicholas's mother, the Dowager Empress Marie. Having survived on a diet of buckwheat and pea soup, she was evacuated on a British warship and taken to Denmark. Although she spent her remaining years bickering with Christian X, her nephew, about the electricity bill, she never accepted that Nicholas and his family had died. She knew, she said, they had not. Furthermore, she knew where they were.

Attempts to explain the true fate of Nicholas's family belong more to the entertainment business than to the world of scholarship. They have inspired a Hollywood film, a wealth of preposterous literature and more people with claims to be survivors than there are White Russians. The majority stem from America, the origin of a belief that Francis Bacon was not only the author of all Elizabethan literature, including the Authorized Version of the Bible, but was also the son of Queen Elizabeth.

In 1919 was published the diary of an anonymous American agent. In it he claimed to have been briefed by the Kaiser before making the journey to Ekaterinburg. Having smuggled the Romanoffs out of a tunnel, he accompanied them on a journey through Tibet, disguised as pilgrims.

In 1923 another American spy, William McGarry, claimed to have met Nicholas on the steps of Notre Dame de la Garde in Marseilles. 'It's good to see you again,' McGarry warmly greeted him, 'but you look pale.'

'I don't feel very well,' conceded the former Emperor and Autocrat of All the Russias. Not surprising, since he had already been spotted by a Swedish bandleader in the Crimea, as a white-haired remnant of his former self in London, and in various locations from Malta to Breslav.

It was from Poland in 1960 that his son and heir materialized, having been first spotted in northern Iraq forty-four years before. He was disguised as Michael Goleniewski – a lieutenant-colonel in Polish Intelligence and a double-agent known to the West as 'Sharpshooter'. New York took him to its credulous bosom, and he now writes a newspaper column under his Imperial by-line.

Three years later his 'sister', a Chicago housewife known as Eugenia Smith, turned up at a publishing house and revealed that she was Anastasia – whereupon the Grand Duchess Maria promptly surfaced in Warsaw. Her father, she said, brandishing a photo of Nicholas as a Polish tram-driver, had died peacefully in 1952. The photo was examined by experts. They acknowledged the snapshot bore many resemblances to a Polish tram-driver.

There is one claimant, however, over whom the imperial mist still lingers. Seventeen months after Anastasia's escape from Perm, in February 1920, a twenty-year-old girl was hauled out of the Landwehr

Canal in Berlin. She had tried to take her own life. After two years in a mental ward she was recognized by a fellow patient as the Grand Duchess Anastasia. When this was put to her, she agreed it was indeed the case. She had survived the massacre, been rescued by a soldier – one Alexander Tschaikovsky – with whom she had travelled in a farm cart to Bucharest, and there had given birth to his son.

There followed a forty-eight-year battle to prove her identity; a battle which resulted in one of Germany's longest running court cases, and the verdict, on 17 February 1970, that her claim was 'neither established nor refuted'.

The most significant fact about this affair – apart from the passions evoked and the expense incurred – was the hysterical reaction of surviving Romanoffs and the neat division between her supporters and opponents. Those for numbered the Kaiser's second wife, Louis Ferdinand's mother and Nicholas II's mistress. The girl looked and spoke like Anastasia, had the same handwriting, the same scar on her shoulder from a cauterized mole and the same enlarged big toe. What was more, when given a list of questions to which the real Anastasia alone would have known the answers, she not only gave the correct reply but added details. She even reminded an officer she had nursed in 1916 of a nickname coined by her for an elderly colonel. The officer had forgotten it until then.

For her opponents, forcibly led by the Grand Duke Ernst Ludwig of Hesse, 1916 is the crunch date. In 1925, when asked about the last time she had met her Uncle Ernie, the girl answered 'in the war, with us at home'. On hearing of this, the Grand Duke categorically refused to involve himself. It is not hard to see why. This was the first time an allusion had been made to his St Petersburg visit. With the German Secret Service bidding to re-establish monarchy, it was hardly the most opportune time to admit that he had been consorting with the enemy. X.7. might just as well have stayed at home.

Uncle Ernie was joined by a formidable array of non-believers, including Lord Mountbatten, the Marchioness of Milford Haven and twelve members of the Romanoff family. In October 1928 a document bearing their signatures was released from the Grand Duke of Hesse's court. It spoke of the Imperial Family's 'unanimous decision' that Anastasia was 'not the daughter of the Tsar'. The twelve signed on behalf of the forty-four surviving members of the Romanoff family. Of the twelve, only one – Grand Duchess Olga – had set eyes on her. It was Olga who after their first meeting had said, 'my reason cannot grasp it but my heart tells me that the little one is Anastasia.'

As one White Russian put it, 'even if she *is* Anastasia, this affair must be defeated in the interests of the Russian monarchy'. If it was best that the Romanoffs remained martyrs and the Bolsheviks murderers, it was to no good that a member of the Imperial Family might have survived – especially if she had given birth to the bastard of a Polish-Bolshevik soldier.

'Anastasia', better known as Anna Anderson, was never certified as insane, which is perhaps surprising since most of her life was spent in having to return again and again to a childhood even more pathological than that of Dr Habsburg. 'One becomes ill when one must again and again repeat,' she complained, her handkerchief pressed to her mouth – though it was unfortunate that evidence used to support her escape from Russia sometimes conflicted with her account of that night in July 1918. Nevertheless, it seemed unlikely she was pretending. After treating her for eight months, the director of Stillachhaus sanatorium in Bavaria maintained, ' . . . it is absolutely out of the question that this woman is deliberately playing the part of another, and [furthermore] that her behaviour when observed in its entirety does not in any respect gainsay that she is the person she says she is.'

After living off sympathetic aristocrats for some time, Anna made for America. She seemed more interested in parakeets and cats than in helping supporters lay claim to the alleged Romanoff fortune. In 1968 she married a history professor in Virginia. As Mrs John E. Manahan, she lives quietly in a suburb of Charlottesville.

Just as the family divided ranks over Anna Anderson's identity, so have they feuded with each other on the subject of Nicholas's successor. His prophecy has come true. 'In the end I fear a whole colony of members of the Russian Imperial Family will be established in Paris with their semi-legitimate and illegitimate wives.' His cousin, Grand Duke Cyril, was the senior male to leave Russia. Banished by Nicholas for marrying a divorced woman without his consent, the former wife of Grand Duke Ernst Ludwig of Hesse, Cyril later managed to escape the Bolsheviks by fleeing across the ice into Finland. In 1924 he proclaimed himself Emperor and Autocrat of All the Russias, and his son Vladimir, his heir. In 1925 he drafted a new constitution and sat down to await the hour when his people would recover their sanity. It couldn't be long, he thought. In the woods near Paris, two thousand Imperial officers roared at the sight of him, 'The day of glory is near!' Evidently, it was not.

The only Romanoffs not to swear allegiance to Cyril were those who had been evacuated from the Crimea. Apart from the Dowager Empress Marie, they included Grand Duke Nicholas, the former commander-in-chief of the army, his brother, Grand Duke Peter, and Peter's son Roman. They represented the next senior line, being descendants of Tsar Nicholas I, and they reckoned it was up to the Russian people to choose what régime they wanted.

This rift was inherited by the next generation. Cyril's son Vladimir is the undisputed genealogical head of the family. He has certainly acted in the autocratic manner of his ancestors. (Like Peter the Great, who worked in a Deptford shipyard, Vladimir used the name Mikhailov during a stint at a factory in Peterborough.) In power, the finer points of dynastic law can be tailored on request. In exile they become all-important, and it is the conflicting interpretation of this law which has caused the trouble.

The main stumbling block appears to be Vladimir's appointment of his daughter, Maria, as heiress – despite a tradition that the claim should pass with his death to the next senior male. When Vladimir created Maria's German husband a Grand Duke there was a further outcry, and five powerful Romanoffs condemned this unwarranted act. According to David Williamson, compiler of the pedigrees in *Burke's Royal Families of the World* – and a man 'very favourably inclined' towards Anna Anderson – 'most of the other members of the family, and indeed a lot of White Russians living in exile . . . would prefer to regard Prince Nicholas Romanoff as the head of the family.'

Prince Nicholas is the son of Prince Roman and the grandson of Grand Duke Peter. He is married to a beautiful Florentine Countess, whose family are mentioned in Dante, and divides his time between a flat in Rome and a 600-acre farm on the coast near Florence. As he drove me north from Rome to this estate, he expanded warmly on every subject under the sun.

'I don't believe she is Anastasia, but that's only my personal conclusion,' he said as we left the capital. 'I have no proof, but I respect her because after all she worked very hard at it. Whatever the case she deserves to be regarded as the Grand Duchess.'

His own life story followed as we snaked through the hills round Porto

Santo Stefano. 'I am stateless,' he boasted. Born in the South of France, he remembered the Romanoff elders at dinner talking about St Petersburg and their estates 'as if they were still existing. "God, the garden must be going to the dogs, and the house too with the east wing burning down." You know, that sort of thing.' During the war, he had fled from the Germans to Rome, and to the umbrage of his great-aunt, Victor Emmanuel's wife. He was still there when the King fled and the Germans occupied the city. 'We practically stayed indoors for eight months. When we first managed to get out, I didn't know how to walk on the street.' With the coming of the Allies, Nicholas got himself a job with the military. 'It sounds very grand, but in fact I was minding typewriters and teleprinter machines.' He spent four years sowing his oats in Egypt, married his Countess and has led a life in the past thirty years of an Italian country squire. At his farm near San Vicenzo, deep in a pine forest, he occupies himself in painting watercolours, shooting wild boars and painting watercolours of himself shooting wild boars. The rooms are littered with tusks and heads and frescoes of the chase. He explained one of his creations to me. 'A very curious thing happened to me once. I was standing on a rocky ledge and suddenly I heard a noise above me, and naturally I went like that — ' He raised an imaginary shot-gun. 'And there was a wild boar peering at me from about two metres over my head. I didn't know what to do. I couldn't shoot it – the damn thing would have fallen on top of me.'

Nicholas also paints battleships. He could name every vessel at the battle of Jutland, he said proudly – and then produced a less serious project, a story in cartoons of a circular iron-clad gunboat. It had sailed around the world for seventy years without its crew having the faintest idea of the revolution at home . . . He has two relics of Empire: the standard carried by his great-uncle Nicholas, the tall, white-bearded commander of the Russian army; and, above the fireplace, the Imperial arms, prised from the doorway of some consulate.

'The Romanoffs were never Russian noblemen, you know,' he said, holding a glass of vodka. 'And I am perhaps the least noble of all Romanoffs because I have too much Montenegran shepherd's blood.' It gave him an appearance as healthy as his outlook.

'Strangely enough, I'm not a monarchist, because that means I presume in advance that monarchy is the best solution for any problem anywhere, any place, any time. There are moments in history when other solutions are advisable. Of course, the advantages are that you don't have to re-elect the King. He's always around. He has no interest in promoting himself year in, year out. It's an extremely convenient solution so that politicians can do their work.'

What were the chances of restoration? He chuckled. 'I don't think it's quite likely at this moment, but history has such strange quirks that anything can happen.'

What did it then mean to be royal?

'Royal is such a terrible expression really. It more or less implies that being in exile we wear uniforms and decorations and orders. It's not that. It's the dignity of a family. It's name, it's tradition. And they can be very well preserved and kept in a blue shirt.'

Since his father's death in 1978, and the growing schism with cousin Vladimir, Nicholas has concerned himself with maintaining this tradition. As demonstrated by the Russian Orthodox wedding, royalty is a symbol of the family. A crown is placed on the head of both partners to show they are prince and princess of their own hearth. For several years, Nicholas has been custodian of the Romanoff Family Association. Its aim is 'to unite the family which is scattered all over the world, and have every Romanoff know the family's history. But absolutely no politics. We are not concerned with dynastic matters.'

There are thirty-three Romanoffs in total. They have dispersed to Australia, San Francisco, British Columbia, France, Denmark and Italy. Nicholas has traced them all except one, another Nicholas, who was last heard of working as a petrol pump attendant in Idaho. 'An excellent occupation, but we can't find him.' Disappearance seems to be as much a family tradition as argument. The day is not far off when a man in a boiler-suit will turn up and stake his claim to be Prince Nicholas, son of Rostislav.

PART THREE
ROYAL VARIETY

10

How to be a King

'I am asked to inquire whether under any circumstances you would consider accepting the dignity of Kingship for Albania.'

LETTER TO FIRST EARL OF INCHCAPE, 29 OCTOBER 1921

The fall of a dynasty is one thing, but what about its roots? How does a man become a king? Does he really need to be a son of God or a child of the sun? Certainly in the last two centuries this has not necessarily been the case. In 1862 Lord Stanley, later Earl of Derby, indignantly rejected an offer of the Greek throne. Were the Greek people unaware that he was to be the next Earl of Derby? Lord Rothermere, it will be remembered, was approached with the Hungarian throne; and in 1920 the Albanians were looking for 'an English country gentleman with ten thousand a year' – a somewhat ironic requirement since it perfectly described the life-style of most deposed monarchs.

One such candidate was Lord Inchcape. A story goes that one day in October 1921 a special messenger arrived from London as he was enjoying a family lunch at his castle in Ayrshire. His butler interrupted the meal with the following news: 'My Lord,' he said. 'You have just been offered the throne of Albania.' Lord Inchcape's alleged reply bore all the qualities of an English aristocrat. 'Where is it?' he asked.

Not until a letter appeared next day was the offer believed. It was signed by the English representative of big Balkan interests.

> I do not know whether this is the first time in your career that you have been offered a Kingdom, and I fully realize of course this is a matter that you could not consider seriously, especially in view of the fact that the new King would be expected to do all in his power financially and

politically to help in the construction of Railways, Roads, Schools and Public Buildings throughout the country . . . Perhaps next time you are cruising in the Mediterranean you would feel drawn to put in at Valona or Durazzo in order to express your sentiments, whatever they may be, in connection with the offer which I am now seriously putting before you. In any case, if you turn it down entirely perhaps you would feel called upon to suggest the name of some wealthy Englishman or American with administrative power who would care to take up the cudgels on Albania's behalf, thereby securing an honourable position as Albania's King.

Lord Inchcape was concise in his reply. 'It is a great compliment to be offered the Crown of Albania, but it is not in my line!'

Other contenders included Colonel Aubrey Herbert, on whom John Buchan based the character Greenmantle, and the cricketer, C.B. Fry. While visiting a Balkan dignitary in Geneva, as he enjoyed his breakfast in bed, Fry was asked if he would like to be King of Albania. 'I accepted on the nail. I was willing to be King of any willing nation.' He was the odds-on favourite for a fortnight, but probably scuppered his chances by diverting too much whisky down the throat of the Albanian bishop who was despatched to assess him.

When the press carried reports that a throne was up for grabs, there was a deluge of applications. Among those who submitted their curricula vitae were a naval cadet and a dancing instructress. The chances of such hopefuls were about as likely as the journalist Bernard Levin becoming King of Flunubria. It was a title granted him in a letter of citation by the comedian Peter Sellers. 'I know there is no such place as Flunubria at the moment, but if there should be, you will be ready to take over.' When he does King Bernard's first act will be to chop off the heads of children who follow in their father's profession. His dynasty promises to be short-lived.

For those not born into the purple, it is by no means easy to enter the charmed circle. In September 1893 James Aloysius Harden-Hickey, the son of an Irish gold-digger, proclaimed himself James I of Trinidad, a minute island off the Brazilian coast inhabited only by wild pigs and goats. His Highness opened a Chancery in New York which painted a picture of a land rich in guano on the surface and in hidden treasure beneath it (Trinidad apparently was the burial site of treasure stole from Lima

Cathedral in 1825). No one took any notice of Harden-Hickey and in 1898 His Highness committed suicide in Texas.

Another James I was a wealthy sugar manufacturer called Jacques Lebaudy who styled himself Emperor of the Sahara. In 1903 Lebaudy landed near Cape Juby on the Spanish territory of Rio de Oro. The Imperial Family and staff were installed in tents while their future capital of Troja was pegged out. Concluding from a thorough survey of the local terrain that a horse was incapable of adapting to the sands while a camel lacked the necessary speed, Lebaudy ordered a portable stable to be sent from England. In it he planned to cross the two strains and produce a hybrid, built for endurance and speed, called a 'cha-val'. Unfortunately bankruptcy overtook Sa Majesté Jacques Ier Empereur du Sahara before either his empire – or his animal – could be consolidated. There are, however, men tempted by the lure of a crown who have been able to found kingdoms and dynasties every inch as valid as those founded by Habsburgs and Braganças. One such was another James, the first White Rajah of Sarawak.

James Brooke began his glamorous life as the son of a High Court judge in Benares. He spent his childhood ping-ponging between India and England, where he was educated at Norwich Grammar School and became the despair of a history tutor. 'Do you not want to learn how countries have been made?' 'No,' replied James prophetically. 'I would much rather make one of my own.'

In 1825, while serving in the Indian army on a mission against the Burmese, he received a bullet in his lung. (Some say it was his genitals, which was why he never married.) He returned to England to recuperate. Resigning his commission, and spending his father's modest fortune on a 142-ton schooner, called, appropriately, *The Royalist*, James set sail again for the East with a motley crew of twenty. His vague aim was to inspect the island of Borneo and see if a settlement could be founded in the area.

Dropping anchor at Singapore in the summer of 1839, he heard tell of an Anglophile leader who was having a spot of bother with some rebels in a western province of Borneo. The settlement, known as Cerava by its Portuguese discoverers, was called Sarawak. Having loaded *The Royalist* with a cargo of gaudy silks and preserved ginger, James made for Kuching, the capital, where the delighted Rajah presented him with an orang-utan –and begged him to stay and help quash the rebellion. 'I could not, as an English gentleman, desert him under such circumstances,' James explained tellingly. A pity he was not born a century later. When he threatened to leave, after realizing that the Rajah's forces were keener to hurl insults than spears, the Rajah tearfully 'offered me the country of Siniawan and Sarawak and its government and trade, if I would only stop and not desert him.' This bait, James confessed, 'was a tempting one'. Armed with a cutlass and followed by his crew, he set out for the enemy stronghold. Casting eyes on someone who at last meant business, the rebels surrendered. A four-year war was over, and James was given due credit. 'He is the rain and the sun and the moon of our existence,' the natives chanted, beating their muffled drums. The Rajah's overlord, the Sultan of Brunei, agreed. (He was a mental defective with an extra thumb on his right hand.) Accordingly, on 24 September 1841, James Brooke was declared Rajah and Governor of Sarawak, 'amidst the roar of cannon and a general display of flags and banners from the shore and river.' Anyone who disagreed with his accession would have their skull cleft.

'I have at last a country,' James told himself, settling into a wood-and-matting chalet at Kuching. 'But, oh, how ravaged by war, how torn by dissension and ruined by duplicity, weakness and intrigue.' From then on, his dream was to enforce order and establish self-government. Promising that murder, robbery and other heinous crimes would be punished according to the *ondong-ondong* – the traditional laws – Rajah Brooke occupied his days in suppressing the main threat to his country. Purchasing another boat, with a similarly appropriate name, *The Jolly Bachelor*, and relying on the help of the Royal Navy, he made repeated expeditions to exterminate the pirates who were destroying Sarawak's coastal trade. On overturning their canoes, he would levy a fine of gongs rather than indulge in the local manner of dealing with an enemy.

Keen as he was not to interfere with native customs, Rajah Brooke did take exception to head-hunting. Unfortunately, it was a deep-rooted addiction among his people. No one could call himself a man until he had taken a head and, such is human nature, no man could impress a woman until he had several of these macabre chestnut-like objects dangling from his verandah. After being smoked and bound in rattan, each head would be fed with rice and a fat cigar pushed between the dry lips.

In 1847 Rajah Brooke sailed for England. Four years previously he had offered Sarawak as a protectorate to the government, but they were not interested in a land of believers in omens and the flight of birds. All the same, he received a sort of unofficial recognition on his homecoming. He was a guest of Queen Victoria at Windsor Castle, he was created a Knight of the Bath, and though not received as Rajah, he was appointed consul-general for Borneo.

During the last years of Brooke's rule, his day-dream of advancing the Malayan race went slightly sour. In Westminster a number of Radicals felt he was too quick to label his opponents as pirates – although people sent out to investigate soon had their heads cut off by those whose existence they denied. A Committee of Inquiry exonerated Brooke, but under-mined the confidence of his subjects in him. He contracted smallpox, and after his capital had been brutally attacked by a gang of Chinese tin-miners he escaped through his bathroom and returned again to England. In 1864 the British government at last recognized Sarawak as a sovereign state – if not as a protectorate. Funds were low. The Rajah had not found, as he had hoped, a wealth of gold and diamonds in the swamps. He made advances to Belgium, France and Holland, without much success, and died in Devon after an untidy quarrel with his nephews as to who would be his heir.

It was his youngest nephew, Charles Brooke, who succeeded him in 1868 as the second White Rajah of Sarawak. A bony-faced man with grey eyes and a large moustache, Charles was in every way different from his uncle. Severe, chilly and aloof, he was an administrator not an adventurer, a man of thrift rather than an entertainer. On his honeymoon, he lavished his poor wife with grizzled chicken legs and ship's biscuits, and though she bore him several children, the marriage was to end when he served up her pet doves in a pie. His manner was made the more intimidating after he rode into a tree and lost an eye. He replaced it with a glass ball destined for a stuffed albatross. Rolling his beady eye over the women of Kuching, he would woo them in atrocious French, to some advantage for, if nothing else, Charles Brooke was absolute monarch of his kingdom. 'Yet thou-sands yet unborn will bless the name of Brooke', went the national anthem of Sarawak, which by his death in 1917 he had turned into a model state.

In a treaty of 1888 the British finally guaranteed Sarawak its indepen-dence. Brooke was able to use this security to replace his capital's wooden houses with stone buildings. He built a railway and a wireless station, and an economy based on an oil well, rubber and pepper plantations and the sale of turtle eggs and birds' nests. Like his uncle, though, he quarrelled with his heir and eldest son, Vyner Brooke. Nor was Sylvia, the last Ranee of Sarawak, who had married Vyner in 1911, in Charles's good books. The bush telegraph spoke of a plot to disinherit them, and he made little secret of his dislike. At one garden party in Kuching, Sylvia felt some drops and said loudly, 'Ooh, it's going to rain.' When she turned round, however, she saw the Rajah relieving himself over the verandah.

Vyner, the last of the ruling Brookes, was no financial genius and a man crippled by shyness. On the day of his coronation, Sylvia had to follow him around with glass after glass of brandy to fortify his spirits before the ceremony. When she did manage to coax him into his uniform, the sleeves dropped off, eaten away by silver-fish. Once he was sworn in as Rajah, she was made to walk four paces behind him and the lackeys who held a yellow umbrella over his head. Two of Vyner's more far-reaching innovations were a constitution giving his people a greater say in the affairs of state, and the Sylvia Cinema, which was inaugurated with a showing of *King Kong*. It was Sylvia's idea to make a film of 'The Great White Rajah' – James Brooke. She wrote a synopsis which was snapped up by Errol Flynn – who had taken up where Louis Ferdinand had left off, and married Lili Damita. The Hollywood actor believed James Brooke must have been rather like him, until Sylvia explained that a wound in India had deprived the first Rajah of Flynn's greatest asset. With no prospect of any love interest, the project fizzled out. So too, shortly afterwards, did the Brooke dynasty. In the autumn of 1941 Sarawak's centenary celebrations were held. Three months later the Japanese invaded.

Vyner spent the war in London. He came to realize that when it was over, Sarawak would need more help than he could give. Moreover he had inherited the congenital Brooke talent for quarrelling with his heirs. Once more he offered his country to the British. They accepted, and on 24 July 1946, Sarawak was annexed to the British Crown.

The transfer was handled shoddily, and did not have the total support of a people who believed that their Rajah would live for ever. In 1949, as the second governor stepped ashore at a village up-river, he was stabbed to death.

The Brooke family were forbidden to return, and Vyner died, impoverished, surrounded by his budgerigars in a dilapidated house in Albion Street, London. A few months later Sarawak was ceded to Malaysia.

Vyner left three daughters. His eight sons-in-law had included an earl, a bandleader, an all-in wrestler and a Spanish fruit-importer. One summer's morning I went to a house off Warwick Avenue in London to meet the man who might be fourth Rajah of Sarawak. Son of the second Earl of Inchcape – the man with a poor sense of geography – and grandson of Vyner, Lord Tanlaw is a short, energetic politician. A former Liberal spokesman on energy, he is first and foremost a realist. He has not very much choice. At his curved desk, in an open blue shirt, he was quick to give credit to a family which had brought peace and prosperity to a far-off slice of Asia.

'There's a great deal to learn from the Brookes, how they governed a multi-national society without any of the paraphernalia of bureaucracy. I'm sure my grandfather was constitutionally wrong in 1946. The Iban lawyers say technically the constitution is illegal. Sarawak cannot be owned by a nation state. It can only be run by members of the Brooke family. He did the only thing possible, though. It had been decimated in the war. And I was too young. I was still at prep school. The Foreign Office did ban any of my family from returning – after the governor was assassinated by the Muslim Brotherhood. But I have been back. The last time was in 1966. I was demonstrating hydrofoil patrol boats. I spent three weeks in the shipyard putting them together. Then I had to judge the Miss Sarawak competition, with bands playing and everything. There were some emotional moments,' he added, trying to keep his pipe alight.

It was suggested to the Macmillan government that Lord Tanlaw might have made a suitable governor. I asked if there was any prospect of him returning in some official capacity.

'I see a possibility of disenchantment, with greed. Sarawak is rich in oil. A movement might come into being for independence using the original terms of the constitution. Being multi-racial, they wouldn't mind who was the head. Obviously, it would be much easier if it was a Brooke. I'm a realist, though. I would refuse to be executive head. I would be under an obligation to accept a non-executive position. But if I had returned like that, someone would have shot me by now. Assassination's part of the game. I wouldn't be here. All the same, my grandfather made sure I was legally his heir and the position will pass to my son. There may come a time when he is needed.'

Lord Tanlaw keeps a low profile in his relations with Sarawak. He does not wish to offend the Malays, who since 1963 have tended to rewrite its history. 'They show films about how bad the Brookes were. They even thought of pulling down the statue of the third Rajah, but the Ibans would have come down the river.' His main link with the country lies in his position as President of the Sarawak Association. Every year, from a fund left by his grandfather, he is able to give scholarships in England to two or three students from Sarawak.

One point continued to intrigue me. 'Yes, head-hunting still goes on. It's illegal, it's a crime, but it happens now and then when law and order break down. The Rajahs used to insist the heads had names, because they were human beings once. I met a little man who had collected about six.' Lord Tanlaw made a comparison with the Gurkhas. He was sure they would have improved their marital prospects no end by cutting off some Argentine heads in the Falklands.

As head of the exiled Royal House of Araucania and Patagonia, Philippe Boiry might not have approved. Were he in power, the Falklands Islands would fall within his jurisdiction.

A few days before the Task Force landed at San Carlos, I visited his small château of La Chèze in the truffling country of Perigord. It was the birthplace of the first king, Orélie-Antoine de Tounens. Like Lord Tanlaw, Philippe Boiry – or the Prince d'Araucanie as he is known on his passport – is a pipe-smoker with a grey moustache. He is also heir to one of the most extraordinary dynasties in the annals of royalty. On a wall in one of La Chèze's airy rooms there is a map of his former territories, and, beneath a clutch of familiar islands the words 'parts of the Kingdom occupied by foreigners but claimed for the Kingdom for geopolitical reasons'. The Prince elaborated. 'They are the natural extension of the Andes, geographically speaking, and therefore of Patagonia. My father always held the title Prince of the Falklands to assert this reclamation. But,' he said, smiling, 'I haven't done anything about it.'

In 1858 the young lawyer and freemason Orélie-Antoine de Tounens left his home in Perigueux and sailed on a British steamer for Chile. Claiming descent from the Gallo-Roman prince, Tonantius Ferreolus – the founder of Tonneins – he wished to restore the lustre to his family name. Fired by the example of Rajah Brooke, he hoped to do so by founding not a town but an empire. The trouble was where? The more he thought about it, the more often South America cropped up. Had not Pizarro, a pig farmer from Estramadura, been able to conquer the whole continent? Had not San Martin, before he died in exile in Boulogne, crossed the Andes with a handful of men and taken Chile? And had not Lord Cochrane planned to free Napoleon from Santa Helena and make him Emperor of South America? Scouring the history books, Orélie – which sounds like a French pronunciation of O'Riley – had come across a territory next to Chile that was to all intents and purposes *res nullius*. It was not difficult to see why. For three hundred years the Araucanian Indians had fiercely defended their lands against the Spanish. In 1557 the Conquistador poet Ercilla lopped the hands off a prisoner who ran screaming back to his camp, showed his bleeding stumps and demanded vengeance. Having seen to it that the Araucanians would from then on resist all conquests, Ercilla returned to Spain and celebrated their independence in an epic poem. 'No king has ever ruled you,' he wrote, 'nor foreign power controlled you.' Until the creation of Chile in 1818, the Spanish were to sign a total of six treaties with the Indians recognizing their autonomy. The situation in 1860 was the same. The Araucanians, admitted one Chilean historian, existed in a state of 'absolute independence'.

What chance, then, had the tall and bearded Orélie-Antoine as he rode along the banks of the Bio-Bio in the autumn of 1860? He was alone, unarmed and penniless, and did not speak much Spanish – or indeed Mapuche. As luck would have it, his arrival was a timely one. For some months the witch-doctors had prophesied the coming of a white stranger who would unite the tribes and lead them to victory against the Chileans. (Myths of a white liberator were common throughout South America. The Aztecs had stupidly mistaken the Conquistadors for emissaries of their exiled god, Quetzlcoatl – whom some people believe to have been a Welshman.)

Orélie's accession as king was consequently assured. 'My Minister of War will give you modern weapons,' he promised in halting Spanish, although no such person existed. 'My Naval Minister will give you ships.' The enthusiasm which greeted this speech, according to his biographer Saint-Loup, was indescribable. Horsemen whooped, their women shrieked and the dogs barked. On 17 November he drafted out a sixty-six-article constitution, modelled on the French constitution of 1852. Three days later a messenger galloped up to say that the tribes of Patagonia would also like to join his kingdom. Thus was Orélie-Antoine I freely elected king by the original inhabitants of two lands which in their entire history had never submitted to foreigners. As Prince Philippe rightly observes, few heads of state can boast such legitimacy.

Soon after, Orélie left for Chile; to proclaim the news to the world, and to instruct a Freemason friend in Perigueux to press the French government for a loan of 50 million francs. Orélie was confident of the outcome. He was offering his country a Nouvelle France, blessed, he wrote, with an excellent climate, without epidemics or wild beasts and riddled with gold and silver mines. All he needed were some people to help him run it. With the loan, his friend was expected to recruit an army of 15,000 men and purchase one warship, two frigates and a pair of corvettes.

The world, however, was unimpressed, as was the French government. Neither money nor recognition was forthcoming – just some sarcastic reports in the French press about how this venture gave the same amount of confidence as Orélie inspired in his former clients.

Ridiculed and rejected, he returned to his people, bearing a lot of green, white and blue flags, the new colours of his kingdom. Again, the enthusiasm was boundless. Mounted troops galloped round him shouting, 'Long live the union of all tribes under the same head and the same flag!' As he relaxed on a hide bed strung between four posts, Orélie reflected that just because it was held in the open and on horseback, his parliament was no less a parliament. From that day forth, he ordered, whenever his name was mentioned, people should bare their heads.

It was too good to last. With a possible 30,000 men at his disposal, Orélie was becoming more than a thorn in Chile's side. In January 1862, while riding to his capital, Angol, he was betrayed by an interpreter and during his siesta was captured by the Chilean authorities. He spent a year in a prison cell. His hair fell out and he suffered a case of chronic dysentery. It was said that he only gained his freedom and repatriation at the discreet intervention of Napoleon III, who had always dreamed of an empire in the Americas. An attempt had been made to certify him as mad. If he was mad, wrote Saint-Loup, it was in the manner of Cortes, Magellan and Scott.

A man of uncommon destiny and courage, Orélie was also dogged by an unusual run of bad luck. In 1869 he reappeared on the Rio Negro and spent two years at the head of his troops fighting the Chileans, who had by now put a price on his head. After appointing five chieftains to his cabinet, and decorating them with an order called the Couronne d'Acier, he sailed for France in search of yet more funds – and a wife.

In the latter, he was unsuccessful. An advertisement was placed for a young girl of good health and character, from an honest and respectable family and endowed with all the qualities of a 'perfect queen'. The only response was that of hilarity. He did, nevertheless, manage to secure the support of a French bank.

In 1874 Orélie disembarked at Bahia Blanca disguised in dark glasses as Jean Prat. He had with him three accomplices – purporting to work for the Nicolas Cordier Bank in Paris – and a suitcase of coins embossed with his head. He was recognized almost immediately, not by the Indians, but by an Argentine colonel on his way to a bridge club. That night armed police surrounded 'Jean Prat's' lodgings and trained a searchlight on his room until dawn. When questioned, he said he didn't know Orélie, but funnily enough someone once before had mistaken him for the same person. He spent another four months in jail.

Two years later, Orélie was back in Patagonia, but before he could achieve anything, he went down again with dysentery. After being fitted with an artificial silver anus, he returned to France for the last time where he died in a village near Perigueux in 1878.

Until the end of the last century, captains loading their nitrate cargoes along the Chilean coast would be approached by Indians claiming to be Orélie's natural sons. They spoke of a treasure he had buried on the banks of the Bio-Bio. They wanted a free trip to France. Had any made the journey, they would have discovered a successor already appointed by Orélie – one Gustave Laviarde, a wealthy balloonist and friend of Verlaine, who renamed himself Achilles I. In 1880 this corpulent, fine-moustached fellow placed an announcement in *Figaro* encouraging any of his subjects resident in France to attend a mass in the first King's honour. It ended like this. ' . . . Ay! Cararken Antoine Ier pegny molouches aucas araucanos tehuelches marry marry! Laviarde.'

Achilles took himself very seriously. He recalled Orélie-Antoine's regret that 'if I was English, if I had revealed to the English public what I have already done, the difficulties I have fought against would have been solved a long time ago!' In 1882 Achilles tried to amend this state of affairs. He sailed to England and appointed one Sir Joseph Blech KC his consul-general and financial agent. Blech put his house at 70 Cornhill, London, at Achilles' disposal and promised to raise a loan of one million sterling. It would be used to install the King at the risk of war with Chile and Argentina. Little is known of Blech's enterprise, but it illustrates Achilles' style of government. Better heeled than Orélie, he devoted his fortune to diplomacy rather than action. In a reign of twenty-five years, spent firmly in France, he appointed some 260 consuls throughout the world and gained belated recognition from people like the Shah. Though he was to survive a stick of dynamite thrown under his car, Achilles' death coincided with the effective end of his empire. In 1902 Edward VII of England arbitrarily partitioned the lands of Araucania-Patagonia between Chile and Argentina. In France, however, the flame flickered on, under such men as Antoine II (personal physician to the last Emperor of Brazil) and finally, Prince Philippe.

Since 1951, the Prince has worked hard to rehabilitate his predecessors. He has founded an academy of Araucanian studies, he has hopes of recording the national anthem – composed by one Guillermo Frick in 1864 – and he has vigorously defended his dynasty against all calumnies. Court cases and legal theses attest to the validity of the monarchy and medals meted out to staunch republicans like Eisenhower and Peron have been received with gratitude, not to say enthusiasm. Even the first men on the moon sent a photograph signed with their best wishes.

Prince Philippe has taken it upon himself to renovate the house of La Chèze and maintain the graves of the first two kings at the nearby village of Tourtoirac. We followed the signposts to their tombs. In the graveyard, above the inscription to Orélie, there was an odd-looking crown. 'The mason didn't have a model to go on, so he used one from a pack of cards, the king of hearts. The actual crown was stolen about twenty years ago.' As I paid my homage, I asked if he felt that it was important to maintain the family tradition. 'The answer is simple. When a monarchy is set up, so are some rights which remain permanent. Therefore we have to represent them and if necessary defend them.' He has a dozen representatives abroad – particularly strong in Houston and Guatemala – who lobby for the rights of ethnic minorities in southern South America. The campaign of Rosas and Roca in the nineteenth century sought systematically to exterminate them, but there are, the Prince guesses, anything up to 200,000 Indians left. Though he has not yet visited the area, his work is appreciated by them. Only recently he received a letter of tribute from the main Argentine tribal leader; and not long ago he discovered some sticks of maize beside Orélie's mossy tomb. They were wrapped in a piece of paper on which was scribbled in Indian the words 'Don't forget us'.

There is little fear of that. In the evening, at an oatmeal-coloured château above a river, I attended a reception in his honour, along with members of his court in exile. 'It is hard to make decisions alone,' he confessed, from a

126

cloud of smoke. The men he relied on were an eccentric bunch who carried Araucanian titles like the Marquis de Maden and the Comte de Queilen-Cura. Obviously, a lot of money had been spent on medals. (Even the janitor in the local museum had one, 'Moi, je suis monarchiste,' he had announced proudly.) The Chancellor of the kingdom – whose tight clumps of hair reminded me of the Patagonian scrublands – was decorated like a Christmas tree. He wore silver cuff-links with Philippe's younger face ('only ten have these'), a large Order of the Southern Star ('only thirty have these'), and a tie-pin ('only three have this').

Needless to say the Falklands took up most of the conversation. After a toast to the Prince and to 'l'Araucanie libre', I was taken aside by another member of the court. He was, he explained, a cousin of the Comte de Bougainville, a descendant of the first settler on the islands. He had, he said, the only solution to the problem. Philippe should go out, raise the white, green and blue flag and toss a coin on an annual basis to decide who would govern. At the time I was somewhat sceptical. Having taken another look at what Orélie-Antoine de Tounens achieved in four days, I am now less sure that it was such a bad idea.

My favourite story about royalty is the one least likely to be true. It concerns a young man in the 1920s who pestered *The Times* offices in London to make him their stringer in Albania. Initially they refused. Albania was the most primitive nation in Europe and they had no need of a journalist there. The young man would not relent. He spoke Albanian, he pressed; he knew the country. At length they gave way and off he went. Soon after, Albania hit the headlines. Other papers carried reports of dramatic coups. *The Times* despatched a wire requesting copy. No copy came. Another cable was sent with the same result. By now there was exasperation at the lack of news. A final message warned that unless some material was received by return, the young man would be replaced as *The Times* Albania correspondent. This solicited a reply, albeit brief. 'All is quiet in Albania,' it read. 'I am King. Zog.'

The flamboyant King Zog has inspired more apocryphal stories than probably any other monarch – which is not to belittle his achievement. For two thousand years, Albania and its people, offspring of the Etruscans and Alexander the Great, had been subjected to foreign rule. In 1913 it finally gained independence, and though the first king, a German prince and uncle to Carol of Romania, only lasted six months, Albania's autonomy was guaranteed at the end of the First World War. It was then that Ahmed Bey Zogu appeared on the scene. A soldier and an intellectual with flaming red hair and a face like Salvador Dali, Zogu rose to become Prime Minister at the age of twenty-seven and President by the time he was thirty. In 1928 he was declared King Zog the First (and probably the last) of Albania, the youngest kingdom in Europe.

The ten years, ten months and ten days of his autocratic rule were the most stable in the country's history. He banned polygamy, improved the educational and transport systems and established an effective police force trained by British officers. (His bodyguard was a certain 'Battler' Smith.)

Zog's one vice was gambling. A story is told of some English business-men who visited the capital, Tirana, in the 1930s. After a lengthy foray in search of night-life, they retired defeated to their hotel room and started playing poker. Half an hour later a policeman burst in. They had been observed gambling, he explained. The King himself had spotted them from his palace through a powerful pair of binoculars. The men prepared themselves for the worst as the policeman continued. If they had nothing else lined up that evening, would they like to join His Majesty for a game?

King Zog's rule came to an abrupt end three days after the birth of his son and heir, Crown Prince Leka. On Good Friday 1939, flushed with his Ethiopian campaign, Mussolini invaded and proclaimed Victor Em-manuel King of Albania. Shortly beforehand, loudspeaker vans had driven through Tirana's streets announcing the forthcoming attack and warning everyone to take refuge in their cellars. Towards nightfall when nothing had happened, the bolder spirits thrust their heads outside. They found that not only had the King disappeared, but so had his treasury.

This foresight was to make Zog one of the richest monarchs in exile. When he appeared in June 1940 at the London Ritz, after a journey through Turkey and France and a night spent in the Great Western Hotel, Padding-ton, he carried with him a lot of heavy luggage. Did it contain anything of value, asked the porter? 'Yes,' answered Zog, with perhaps the terseness he had employed when a journalist. 'Gold.' (Apparently he once tried using his gold to become proud purchaser of his formal journal, *The Times*. But, he warned, 'I won't give a penny more than ten million for it.' In those days clearly not enough.)

Protected by six tall bodyguards, the Albanian royal family occupied a third-floor suite and used the ladies' cloakroom as their private air-raid shelter. In the following year, Zog repaired to Lord Parmoor's house in

Buckinghamshire, taking a waiter called Max as his butler. From there he travelled on to Egypt (where he became a neighbour of Victor Emmanuel, the man who had usurped his throne), America (where he bought some Long Island real estate with a bucket of jewels) and France, where he died in 1961.

King Leka I, as he was proclaimed in the Hotel Bristol, Paris, is very much his father's son. I was fortunate enough to catch him on a flying visit to London. He was staying with a friend called Colonel Inigo Jones.

'Leka darling', as he was addressed by the Colonel's wife, sat in a cramped study on a white sofa. When he got up, he stood almost seven feet tall. He had a bloodhound's face with slanting, sad eyes devoid of sadness, a large chin and a small mouth that pouted meaningfully when he had said something. When he spoke, taking his glasses on and off, it was with a faint South African accent, interspersed with 'Look, you'. He had, he explained, just come from breakfast with Frederick Forsyth whom he was persuading to write a book about his father.

Chain smoking from a Thai cigarette-case engraved with a trumpeting elephant, King Leka made it abundantly clear that he was a man of action. Not for him an easy retirement in Estoril or a life of obscurity. 'I am primarily a military animal,' he said. 'I would respond militarily rather than politically or diplomatically. I was born with my ideas focused on one thing – Albania, and how to free it.'

His childhood, of which only three days were spent in Albania, was peripatetic to say the least. After two years at Sandhurst, where he learnt 'what questions to ask', he became an observer on the side of security forces in Vietnam, Thailand and Mozambique. He became a specialist, not an expert. 'X is an unknown quantity; spurt is a drip under pressure.' During the 1960s he used the knowledge he had gained to build up his own paramilitary organization, and financed the men's training through the sale of tractors, cranes and harbour equipment. Contrary to popular opinion, he claims to have been involved in only one arms deal, between the Spanish government and the Saudi Arabians. The number, and where-abouts, of his men is a jealously guarded secret because 'I've been suckered a couple of times.' One suspicious agent asked for a transmitter and some guns. He went to Albania on a recce, but Leka's men followed him. He turned out to be working for the KGB. 'We let him go. And he sent me a card from Moscow. Moscow didn't realize how wide our net was. Nor did we know how big was Moscow's operation.'

From 1962, Leka based himself in a fortress outside Madrid. In 1975 he became the Commander-in-Chief of the Council for the Liberation of Ethnic Albania. It was, he admits, 'like hiding behind your own finger'. That year his operation 'went militant'. He took certain military actions which were basically terrorist, but so carefully planned that they would not cause loss of life – just show that he was a force to be reckoned with. An M72 rocket was fired at the Albanian Embassy in Paris. There were no casualties. The telegraph and telex services between Albania and Western Europe were cut, 'for which we needed frogmen. Frogmen,' he added impressively, 'are difficult to get.' In his last bid to excite interest, Leka had one of his platoons materialize at King Zog's grave in France. After posing for photographs in their uniforms, the troops disappeared into thin air.

In 1977 Leka achieved a notoriety of sorts when he was imprisoned by the Thai government on a charge of arms smuggling. He denied the charge, but boasts that the experience was useful. 'My son,' he had once been told by the Tunisian President, 'if you spend eleven years in prison, that will make you a statesman.' Leka sent a telegram on his release. 'Will six days in prison give me the aspirations of being a statesman?' A return cable bore the word 'Yes'.

Leka's brand of statesmanship, like his life-style, does not readily induce trust. 'I'm not a nutcase . . . or rather I may be, but at least I'm a pragmatic one.' Though there are more Albanians living abroad than at home, he can only count on the active support of some 50,000 political émigrés – who are crippled by in-fighting – and, anyway, everything has been put on ice since he was expelled from Spain in 1979. At his house near Madrid, police had discovered a large cache of arms; they refused to accept that it was for his own protection. With a pistol at his hip and grenades hanging from his belt, Leka flew to Rhodesia and on to South Africa, where he now lives on a farm near Randberg. Since 1979 finance and business have dried up. 'I'm feeling the pinch,' he said, taking off his glasses.

But Leka is a man of limited optimism. If he is acting the part of an absolute monarch in exile, it is so that one day he can play the role of a constitutional monarch in power. When the ice melts and Albania is freed from Communist rule, he will hold a referendum for his people to decide whether they want a monarchy or a republic. If a monarchy, King Zog's constitution of 1928 could provide a starting point. King Leka is understandably a little rusty on certain points of this constitution, such as how often elections are held. In exile there are things that even kings forget.

11

The Pretenders

'As plain Harry Domela I should not receive such attentive service as if I adopted some Baron's title.'

HARRY DOMELA

In the nursery, everyone would like to be the king of some castle. For those who are neither born royal, nor live to find a foreign field where they may be treated as such, there is only one thing to do. Pretend. The history of popular delusions is best charted by looking at a list of impostors to existing thrones.

No country is without its share of Anastasias and Sebastians. Until he was detected and executed, Agrippa's slave not only concealed his master's death, but assumed his position. His fate was that of Perkin Warbeck, who pretended to be one of the Princes in the Tower. Lambert Simnel, a baker's son, got so far as to be anointed and crowned. Though Dublin accepted him as Edward VI, London did not. He ended up as a turnspit in the royal kitchens. In Russia, a hotbed of mushroom monarchs, there were at least four false Demetriuses and six pseudo Peters, while the number of men claiming to be the son of Louis XVI exceeded thirty. The most colourful was one Eleazar Williams, a missionary who surfaced in America. As an imbecilic ten-year-old he had been placed in the care of an Iroquois settlement at Ticonderoga. Four years later, after being struck on the head by a stone, his memory was restored. He was Louis XVII, he realized, the legitimate heir to the throne of France. He had most certainly not – as everyone suspected – died of scrofula in Paris. Once Eleazar's ancestral pride was aroused, he refused to resign all his rights and titles in favour of Louis Philippe. It is not thought that the Bourgeois King lost much sleep over this.

The twentieth century has been enlivened by the antics of a demobilized soldier called Harry Domela. In 1926, unable to find work or lodgings in post-war Berlin, he decided to adopt a Baron's title. It worked wonders. At an art exhibition in Erfurt he was mistaken for Louis Ferdinand's brother, Prince William of Prussia. The more he denied it, the more people invested him with their own fantasies. Domela gave way, but emphasized that he was travelling incognito. 'Many people see in you the future Emperor and King,' a commercial councillor revealed solemnly. 'What a pity that I was a sham prince,' sighed Domela. An American woman recognized him immediately. 'I can see by your whole manner that you are no "ordinary mortal".' 'Call me simply Prince,' responded Domela. 'I've been accustomed to that for years.'

First-class railway carriages and ducal opera-boxes were put at his disposal, and he was invited to meet the local nobility at a charity fête. An unctuous hotel manager, who had leant head over heels to find him money, was instructed to buy up any table-cloths for sale. 'A young man,' explained Domela agreeably, 'never takes money with him on a journey.'

After accepting an invitation to shoot with the Bluchers – and bagging eight hares – Domela was apprehended. He was thrown into prison, but he had had a good run.

In 1981 I attempted to get in touch with King Hassan I of Afghanistan. After much hard work, I followed a trail that led to the premises of David Henshall, a Wilmslow butcher. Under the title Count of Keshem, he doubled as the personal representative of His Majesty in the United Kingdom. Over the telephone, to a background noise of hearty meat-chopping, I explained to the man who answered that I was to eager to speak with the King. 'It's the King speaking,' boomed the reply.

My experience with King Hassan was somewhat unsatisfactory. He agreed to an interview, but then cried off. When I contacted him again, this time in New York, he was still reluctant to meet me. He said he was tired of press reports accusing him of being a phoney. After a certain amount of persuasion, he once more conceded to an interview. Once more he called it off. In despair, I rang the Wilmslow butcher's and asked for the Count of Keshem. He told me sheepishly that he had reverted to plain Mr Henshall. He had discovered that Hassan was illegitimate, which made his claim, at least in the eyes of Western genealogists, 'embarrassing'. He was no longer Hassan's representative.

There are various worthy institutions in Great Britain which support the cause of monarchy and keep a close watch for potential pretenders. One such is *Burke's Peerage*. David Williamson, the chief contributing editor, is an affable fund of information about royalty. In his office in Walton Street, just round the corner from Harrods, he shed light on this 'extremely dubious' King of Afghanistan. Hassan, he explained, claimed to be the son of Amanullah who had reigned in the 1920s. Though his father was King, his mother was not Queen Soraya. Since, by Islamic law, the King could take as many as four wives – and Hassan claimed to be the son of another wife, descended from the Carys, the Scottish aristocratic dynasty – he considered himself a justified claimant.

In Afghanistan, however, his father was superseded by another branch of the family. The last King, Zaher Shah, was forced into exile in 1973 after a military coup and now lives in Rome.

Though Hassan sends large sums of money to rebels, he has not managed to convince David Williamson of his authenticity. 'He might get a footnote.' Two years ago an American lawyer, introducing himself as the Duke of Kandahar, deposited a large folder in Walton Street. He alleged it contained all the documents Williamson required to prove Hassan's legitimacy. These documents consisted of Christmas cards from Queen Marie José of Italy inscribed 'Dear Hassan'. They were plainly not enough to satisfy the strict rules of British genealogy, 'but he's gone down like a bomb in New York.'

I took the opportunity to ask Williamson about bona fida families who have lost their thrones. Did they become any the less royal?

'In some ways they become more royal. They are jealous to guard their remaining privileges, and their supporters treat them with great deference. One would address them in exactly the same way as if they were reigning. They are accepted by other royal families, to whom they are usually related – there's no crowing, because it might be them tomorrow.'

How long could they continue being royal?

'I think most of them can go on indefinitely, as long as they have supporters and are able to live in a reasonable style.' Evidently the length of a dynasty made no difference. 'A man like the late Shah's father, the first of his family to become Shah, is no less royal to my way of thinking than somebody whose ancestors have reigned for several hundred years.'

One tell-tale sign of status, which Williamson swears by, is what he calls the 'tiara rule'. 'I have a theory that the size of a tiara worn by a princess is in inverse proportion to her importance. In other words, if you see a princess with a tiara about a foot high, she's likely to be the most minor member of the most minor former ruling family. Whereas the princess with a very modest single band is probably the highest princess you could expect to meet.'

The Hassan trail led me to another venerable organ, the Monarchist League. Founded in 1943, the League publishes a journal devoted to learned articles and enjoys as its warcry, 'Monarchy is the best policy'. 'If leadership is a quality still sought after in today's world,' runs one essay, 'the ex-monarchs are more than qualified to provide it.' The Chancellor, The Marquess of Bristol, sends telegrams of congratulations on the occasion of a royal birth, and ends his lively editorials with phrases such as 'GOD BE WITH YOU – I CAN'T ALWAYS' – a farewell, he explains, once given him by some publican shutting up for the night.

It was Michael Wynne-Parker, the Principal Secretary and Receiver-General, who concluded the story of the King of Afghanistan. Apparently Hassan had wished to become a member of the Monarchist League under his full title. His credentials, in the form of a photocopied Christmas card, this time from Prince Albert of the Belgians, were thought to require more thorough examination. Mr Wynne-Parker's researchers immediately set to work. Hassan, they discovered, was a man of Anglo–Indian vintage who had arrived in Britain in 1945. His real name turned out to be Derek Cooper.

A lesser known bastion of the monarchic principle is the Monarchist Press Association, which is run by two elderly sisters in West London. They have no telephone and conduct their more urgent business from a coin-box. At their home in Ealing they produce a series of pamphlets entitled 'Kings of Tomorrow'.

My first encounter with them both was at a meeting in the Kensington Town Hall to commemorate the second anniversary of the Shah's death. Making my way through 'inchallahs' to the front row, I introduced myself to Pam and Margaret Davis. They sat in black veils directly facing a portrait of the Shah. When they lifted their lace, I realized that the Davis sisters were identical twins. Before I could say anything more, the ceremony began. The theme music from *Z Cars* was replaced by Iran's national anthem. Everyone – an audience of about a hundred – stood up.

After several bars the record struck a groove, and was removed. Everyone sat down. The anthem began again, and again people rose to their feet singing lustily. It may have been my imagination, but most seemed only to have mastered the first few lines by heart – or else it was a different version to the one they knew. The singing dissolved into a loud humming, with the occasional shout at a familiar word. As I hummed, a troop of men in uniform marched on to the stage, carrying a flag. They marked time in front of the Shah's portrait. Beside me a woman started shaking. I thought she was laughing. She turned out to be in tears. Meanwhile two girls had lit candles beneath the portrait. They stood to attention while a man advanced to the rostrum. He began what looked like a mournful speech, but the microphone did not work. Another man rushed up the stairs to the left of the stage. He came down a few minutes later proudly brandishing a microphone at the end of a long lead. As he reached the stage, the lead jerked taut. It was not long enough. He ran up the staircase again and returned with a radio-microphone. The speech could begin. As the mournful tones resounded through the hall, an assistant adjusted the volume. The speaker's voice rose and rose until it had reached such a level that all one could hear was feedback. The volume control was frantically tapped. It had stuck. The only decipherable sentence in the whole ten minutes had been that the Shah was a great man. When the speech was over, everyone clapped. Everyone clapped through the next speech, none more fervently than the Davis twins. It was delivered by a severe man with a moustache – in Persian. The main event of the evening was billed as a film about the trial of the Shah's generals. Unfortunately, the cans had not turned up. A replacement was found in the form of a video recording of David Frost's interview with the Shah. When Frost appeared on screen, more people started weeping. It was too much for me.

I learnt subsequently that things had hotted up only after I left. One of the girls standing guard over the Shah's portrait had collapsed with a suspected heart attack. Though she was out cold for fifteen minutes, the show had gone on to its climax – a presentation by Margaret Davis of a framed photograph of the Queen in return for one of the young Shah.

My next meeting with the Davis sisters was less traumatic. At tea in their rectory-like house in Ealing, I was served cakes and cucumber sandwiches which were intended to match the red, white and green of the Iranian flag. Pam would talk non-stop for several minutes. Then Margaret would do the same. The only time I got a word in was when I told them about some of the people I had met, at which they sat perched on the edge of their chairs, their mouths open in rapture. After digesting the Iranian colours, I was shown an extensive library of books and documents concerning every aspect of royalty. Most impressive of all were the fruits of their own labours. The 'Kings of Tomorrow' series included some of the most thorough biographies I had read. In each pamphlet was enunciated the aims of their association: to work for a return to monarchical forms of government abroad by promoting serious study of and research into all aspects of monarchy. And to support Her Majesty Queen Elizabeth II.

The Queen enjoys more support today than probably any other British monarch. To Prince Philippe d'Araucanie, 'British monarchy is a symbol of monarchy for the whole world,' and the reason is clear. 'You have an outstanding Queen.' The Countess of Paris goes one stage further. 'England is lucky to have the Queen, but the Queen is very lucky to have the English people.' Her sentiment is echoed by Dr Habsburg – 'Ah, the wisdom of the British people,' he murmurs – and Prince Nicholas Romanoff, 'The British have always managed to show their monarchs what they wanted. On the other hand, British monarchs have always understood extremely clearly what their people wanted.'

That being so, it may come as a surprise to learn that not even the Queen's position is without dispute, and that the more ardent supporters of the Monarchist Press Association could find themselves working at cross-purposes.

It was the banished Stuart kings who for more than a century posed the most dangerous and legitimate threat to their Hanoverian successors. The Stuarts had the misfortune to pick wives who were less fruitful than their mistresses. When that Merry Monarch, Charles II, died without issue from his Portuguese wife Catherine of Bragança, the throne passed to his lascivious brother, James II. 'Dismal Jimmy's' reign was short and none too sweet. The Duke of Monmouth, an illegitimate son of Charles by Lucy Walter, immediately tried to secure the throne for himself. His mother, he claimed, had married Charles when they were living in exile. This made him the rightful heir. No proof was offered, but in 1685 Monmouth proclaimed himself King Monmouth in Taunton, and put a price on James's head. Though the action was to cost him his own, an important document was unearthed at Montagu House in 1879. It was thought to be the marriage certificate of Charles and Lucy Walter. 'That might cause a lot of trouble,' was the Duke of Buccleuch's opinion. He burnt it.

James II's flight in 1688 has been well charted. His wife escaped from London disguised as an Italian laundress, together with their baby son – whom his enemies swore had been smuggled into her bed in a warming-pan. After dropping the Great Seal in the Thames, James followed them to France. Six weeks later his daughter Mary and her hook-nosed husband William of Orange were crowned King and Queen in London. In 1701, the year that James died, an Act of Settlement was passed by one vote. It declared that on the death without issue of William's heir Anne, James's other daughter, the throne would bypass forty-two Catholic claimants for the Protestant heirs of the Electress of Hanover. As James's supporters, the Jacobites, protested, this Act was put into effect by a parliament which had not been called by the legitimate king. It was therefore not a constitutionally legal document.

Nevertheless, when William died after his horse tripped up on a mole-hill in Hampton Park, he was succeeded by Anne. And when in 1714 Anne died, so fat that her coffin was said to be almost square, the Electress's bulbous son, George, took over – or, in Jacobite terms, 'usurped'.

Meanwhile, at the château of St Germain-en-Laye, James's son had been proclaimed by the Pope and Kings of France and Spain as James III of England. In 1715 there was a rising in his name. It fizzled out. Some of his Scottish troops had been more concerned with powdering their hair than their guns. Disconsolate, James moved on to Rome where he married and, amidst a flurry of royal salutes, sired two sons – Charles and Henry.

In 1745, Bonnie Prince Charlie, the eldest, arrived in Scotland having been appointed Regent by his father. He was a brave and dashing figure, but not very literate. In no time at all he had taken Edinburgh and defeated the government troops at Prestonpans. They ran, he wrote, 'like rabets'. Charlie's army pressed on south, taking Carlisle, Lancaster, Manchester and Derby, where, for some reason, his commanders thought it best to retreat. (As George V admitted nearly two hundred years later, 'had Charles Edward gone on from Derby, I should not have been the King of England today'.) Charles was furious. He would refuse to resign his authority 'like an Ideot'. Beset by internecine quarrels, his army was routed at Culloden. For several months Charles hid in the heather drinking whisky. Eventually, disguised in petticoats as Betty Burke, an Irish girl and 'a good spinster', he escaped the redcoats to Rome.

The last years of the exiled Stuart kings are not so bonnie. When James III died, Charles was not recognized by many sovereigns as Charles III – however much support he enjoyed at home. It was said that at George III's coronation, when the traditional gauntlet was flung down challenging the young King's right to the crown, a woman stepped from the crowd and took up the pledge. In its place she left a gauntlet of her own, and a note. If a fair field of combat were allowed, a champion of equal rank and birth would appear and dispute George's claim. 'If England were fairly polled,' said Dr Johnson in the 1770s, 'the present King would be sent away tonight and his adherents hanged tomorrow.'

England was not polled and in Rome Charles III grew fatter and more drunk by the day. In 1772 he married the impoverished Princess of Stolberg. She preferred the company of a young Italian playwright to his own, and despite rumours of a male heir, she died without issue. Charles's claim passed with his death in 1788 to his brother Henry, who had become a Cardinal – an action which put a 'Dager throw' Charles's heart. Henry IX of England asserted his position with a thick Italian accent, but no one took much notice. One Pope was overheard to say that if all Stuarts were so boring, it was not surprising the English had got rid of them. With Henry's death in 1807, the Stuart succession was to become a cause more of embarrassment than honour. The kings of Sardinia were obliged to step in, as the descendants of Charles I's daughter. They had their supporters, though. When Victor I died in 1824, Lord Liverpool wrote to Canning that the nation ought to mourn. 'There are those who think that the ex-King was the lawful King of Great Britain to the day of his death.'

From Sardinia, the Stuart rights were bundled on to the houses of Modena-Este and Bavaria, where they remain to this day.

In Britain the Jacobite cause continued to draw mild if eccentric support. Five people staked their claim as descendants of Bonnie Prince Charlie – either through his mistress or his rumoured male heir. In Scotland at the turn of the century Highland families hung pictures of the latest Stuart Queen, Mary III of Bavaria, and stuck their stamps with George V's head upside down.

Under the heady influence of Walter Scott's novels, a number of clubs began to crop up such as the Order of the White Rose, the Cycle Club, the Society of Sea-Sergeants, and the Legitimist Jacobite League – which in 1891 sought to 'obtain the repeal of the so-called Act of Settlement'. One of the quirkiest was the Forget-me-not Royalist Club. Founded by a Miss Foulds, 'for ladies and girls only', it transpired that half of the forget-me-nots were still at boarding school. Every 30 January they laid wreaths on Charles I's statue in celebration of the fact that 'all right government existeth not by the people but for the people. BY GOD and THROUGH His Divinely Appointed Rulers'. When Miss Foulds died in 1956 she bequeathed a third of her estate to the club. Since she was found to be its only member, she had bequeathed it to herself.

An even more intriguing Jacobite was Captain Wheatley Crow, who would proclaim himself Regent whenever a British king died. Like many sympathizers, he passed his glass across a finger-bowl and drank toasts to the 'King over the water', and 'the little gentleman in black velvet' – the mole whose hill had tripped up William of Orange. Other toasts followed the letters of the alphabet. 'A Blessed Change, Damn Every Foreigner, Get Home James . . . Quick Return Stuart . . .' For good measure a squashed orange might be thrown into the fire.

Some of Captain Crow's accomplices were even more baroque. There was a Prince Paul Salvador of Liverpool, and a man who shot his mistress, the Countess d'Estainville. He went to prison – not the first Jacobite to do so – from where he learned that his beloved Countess was none other than Anna White, a dentist's assistant. In 1926 Captain Crow was instrumental in forming the Royal Stuart Society, an august body which has since become more historical than political. It puts forward no claims on behalf of the Bavarian royal family and in the pages of a regular journal devotes itself to 'the true history of our Stuart Kings and those right principles of monarchy which they in their persons represented.'

Only now and then do Jacobites give way to more than sentiment. A few years ago a woman was arrested by the sergeant-at-arms in the House of Lords. She was busy distributing leaflets in which the Houses of Parliament were accused of being nothing more than illegal conventions. Since 1688 they had not passed a single valid act – nor could they until King Albert I was returned to his throne.

King Albert of England prefers to remain over the water in Munich where he is more commonly known as Duke Albrecht of Bavaria. He regards his position, that of lineal heir of the Royal House of Stuart, as an historical curiosity and the excuse for an occasional joke. 'Are you coming to see me as King of Bavaria or England?' his father wryly asked of a German ambassador to London who had paid him a call.

As a child Albrecht was dressed in Stuart tartan kilts. On the anniversary of Charles I's death he would help fill the rooms of Schloss Nymphenberg with white roses. On the anniversary of James I's death he would accompany his father to lay a wreath at the foot of that king's statue in Munich.

When he dies, the responsibility will pass to his son Prince Franz. A nervous, fine-looking man of fifty who chain smokes from a black holder, Prince Franz sees himself as a figurehead representing the traditions of a small state, with whom people can identify themselves. As the Crown Prince of an unofficial monarchy, his function is to be seen but not heard. His 'Court' numbers an old secretary who was educated at the Convent of the Sacred Heart, Woldingham, and an assistant who is Graham Greene's cousin. And there ends the English connection. As Chairman of the International Council of New York's Museum of Modern Art, Prince Franz is more interested in restoring pictures than restoring his family.

Pretenders to the British throne are not confined to the descendants of James I. In March 1957 a small research team employed by the editor of the *Dumfries and Galloway Standard* made a rather intriguing discovery. They found evidence to suggest that Baron Fitzwalter represented the descendants of Duncan II of Scotland – and could therefore claim precedence over the present royal family who descend from Duncan's younger half-brother David.

In England, Henry VIII nominated the Greys before the Stuarts by his second Act of Succession in 1536. In default of heirs to his son Edward VI, the crown was to pass to the line of Henry's youngest sister Mary, instead of his elder sister Margaret. Edward VI subsequently confirmed this by letters patent. When Henry's spinster daughter Queen Elizabeth died in 1603, this act was nominally in force, and Lord Beauchamp, Mary's senior heir, the legal King. In the event Elizabeth favoured the Stuart line of Margaret.

Potential rebels could make out a case for replacing the present Queen of England with Lord Beauchamp's descendant, Lady Kinloss. A cheerful peeress who spends three days a week in the House of Lords, lobbying for the disabled, she shudders at the thought. 'I wouldn't be Queen for all the tea in China. Besides,' she adds engagingly, if somewhat unfairly, 'I look like the back end of a bus.'

It would have to be an odd-ball who made a case for the least-known, least likely pretender to the British throne. Not surprisingly, perhaps, she lives in Lisbon.

The background to her claim, of which she is unaware, is as extraordinary as her story. On 29 November 1910 a man in his thirties, with black hair, and small features, published an article entitled 'sanctified bigamy' in which he announced that George V's relationship with his wife was 'a sham and shameful marriage'. The man was called Edward Mylius and his periodical, *The Liberator* – 'an international journal devoted to the extension of the republic'. In it he made the following revelation. 'During the year 1890 in the island of Malta, the man who is now King of England was united in lawful wedlock with the daughter of Sir Michael Culme-Seymour, an Admiral of the British Navy. Of this marriage offspring were born.' (George V was then serving in the Royal Navy as the Duke of York. It was not until his elder brother, Prince Albert Victor, died unexpectedly in 1892 that he became heir to the throne and in 1893 married Princess May of Teck.) 'The daughter of Sir Michael Culme-Seymour, if she still lives, is by the unchangeable law of England, the rightful Queen of England and her children are the rightful heirs to the British throne.' A subsequent issue of *The Liberator* pursued this waspishly. 'The *Daily News* of London informs us that the King plans to visit India with his wife. Would the newspaper kindly tell us which wife?'

George V sued for criminal libel. In February 1911 it was proved that the admiral in question had first visited Malta in 1893, three years after the alleged marriage. Of his two daughters, one had never set eyes on the King, while the other had met him twice, the first time in 1879 when she was eight. Nor had the King served on any ship that went to Malta between 1888 and 1893. Mylius wanted the King to come into the dock to give evidence. This he could not do. Mylius was sent to prison. 'I trust,' said George V, 'that this will settle the matter once and for all.'

One of the residents of an old people's home in Lisbon is a spry ninety-three-year-old called Mrs Habsburg Windsor. I had heard something of this woman: that she had once embraced Ricardo Espirito Santo in church having mistaken him for the Duke of Windsor (to whom he bore a passing resemblance), and that in Church she sometimes occupied the British Ambassador's pew, declaring in a guttural German accent that she had the greater claim. This indeed she would have if she was, as she claims, the Queen's great-aunt and daughter to George V and Queen Maria Cristina Habsburg of Spain. Her small room in Rua Gustavos de Mattos

Sequeira is littered with back numbers of the *Spectator* and empty cigarette packets which she had built into a replica of Windsor Castle. On a first brief visit I brought her a packet of Fortnum and Mason's tea, suitably labelled, I thought, with the words 'Royal Blend'. Though she is remarkably alert for her years, Mrs Habsburg Windsor is understandably a little hard of hearing. 'Did you like the pot of tea?' I asked on my next visit, which took place in the home's dark drawing-room. She drew her purple shawl even tighter and a look of horror crossed her face. 'You want to take me to Peking?'

Once I had assured her this was not the case, she told me her story.

'I was born in May 1890 in the Court of Spain. My father was George V. He was not yet King. And my mother was Maria Cristina, the widow of King Alfonso XII. My father Windsor. My mother Habsburg. You see, I can't escape. It was a secret between my father and my mother. It was respected.

'As a baby I was brought by boat to Malta and there a Maltese English lady brought me in a little boat to the middle of the sea to meet one of the ships that were going east. By chance it happened to be going to Smyrna. In Smyrna I was looked after by a Dr Salerio, a very well-known doctor and his wife whom I called godmother. I stayed with them until I was fifteen or sixteen, but during that time I went to the Greek island of Andros and a convent on the Greek island of Tinos.'

She spent two years there and then boarded a ship for Marseilles, from where she followed the railway line to Bordeaux and crossed the border into Spain. After working in music-halls, she married Roberto Cunat, the southern agent (she said 'regent') of a large industrial firm.

It was to be 'many years' before she caught up with her mother. 'I met her once in Madrid. She was with her son, King Alfonso XIII and she looked so happy. I was glad for her because I could imagine the sorrow of being separated from her only daughter.' (She need not have worried. Maria Cristina had given birth to two more.)

'I never spoke about my father with my mother. We had no opportunity. Besides, I think we were both so transported that we never thought of speaking, just of being together. It was an occasion.'

As for her father, Mrs Habsburg Windsor recalls meeting him – as well as her half-brother, the Duke of Windsor – on several occasions; one in particular, following a 'very good visit' George V had made to the Tyrol. He was willing, she said, to do anything for her. What he did is unclear.

More confused still is whether they discussed her status. But she kept the secret until he died. Then, on coming to Lisbon in 1939, she let the cat out of the bag. Nobody took any notice.

I asked Mrs Habsburg Windsor whether she had proof, any birth certificates or 'Christmas cards', any piece of paper. 'You want a piece of paper?' she said, rising from her chair. 'I have one in my room.' I followed in her wake expectantly. The paper she gave me was a blank sheet. Noticing my puzzled expression, she went over to her desk. 'Do you want a pen as well?'

Whether Mrs Habsburg Windsor is a deluded impostor or the illegitimate daughter of George V will probably never be known. There is, however, one footnote of interest. In June 1888 George V as the Duke of York paid a visit to Madrid with the Duke and Duchess of Edinburgh. Their hostess was the Queen Regent, Maria Cristina Habsburg of Spain. . . .

PART FOUR
A CHRISTENING

12

Till Their Kingdoms Come

'I often hear it said and almost every day see it written in the newspapers that "King Alfonso's day is gone" and that "his bolt has been shot", but I invariably add, "Wait and see." '

ALFONSO XIII OF SPAIN

To the grape-pickers in Jerez, southern Spain, the bunch of people who stepped out from the bus and into the Gonzalez-Byass sherry *bodega* must have seemed ordinary enough. Yet this was a package tour with a difference: an informal family outing before the christening next day of twin boys. The boys' father, and the leader of the party, was the Queen's godson, the cheery Crown Prince Alexander of Yugoslavia. Accompanying him in a straw hat was his father-in-law, Dom Pedro, senior claimant to the throne of Brazil; in brown shorts, his slender cousin Princess Elisabeth of Yugoslavia, whose daughter had just starred as the Princess of Wales in an American television drama; the Prince and Princess of Liechtenstein and assorted dukes, duchesses and hangers-on – including Princess Elisabeth's companion, a steely American with a bald patch, and a Greek restaurateur. The only person to remain on the bus was a pink-shirted Baron, a former ADC to Alexander's father. He was suffering from back trouble and consoled himself in the rear seat by looking through a mass of photos relating to King Peter's reign.

Led by Jaime Gonzalez, the group congregated inside the Las Copas *bodega*. It was like entering a cathedral. Under the aluminium domes stretched nave upon nave of oak butts. Each of the 60,000 barrels contained 500 litres of maturing, fermenting sherry. Señor Gonzalez explained the blending process. A barrel on the bottom row would be half emptied and filled with sherry from a barrel on the row above, which in turn would be topped up from the third row, and so on. His audience listened keenly. He could have been describing their own constitution. 'Fantastic,' murmured Alexander. 'Absolutely fantastic.'

Rejoining the Baron in the bus, the group was driven up the hill to the main complex. This time everyone got out. Before lunch, there was a minor ceremony to perform. Filtering through more halls of Tio Pepe and Nutty Solera, Señor Gonzalez ushered his charges into a building known as the 'Kings' Bodega'. Near the entrance, the celebrated Gonzalez-Byass mice provided some amusement. Against four glasses of sweet sherry leant four miniature ladders. Two were occupied by a pair of imbibing rodents.

Besides mice, the building housed barrels which had been signed in white chalk by the company's most famous visitors: Martin Luther King, Cole Porter, Cocteau – and 'Frank Giles of the *Sunday Times*'. It was called the Kings' Bodega because at the far end was a wall of barrels crested with the royal arms of Spain, Portugal and Great Britain (Byass's homeland). Each barrel bore the signature of a monarch. On the rows opposite could be deciphered the names of other royalty such as the Duke of Windsor, Queen Marie of Romania and the Empress of Iran. Only two of the present company, the Princesses of Liechtenstein and Yugoslavia, had not given their signatures. They were handed a piece of chalk and shown a blank lid. By the door the two mice went on drinking obliviously.

Gore Vidal tells how he once accompanied Princess Elisabeth of Yugoslavia to the royal box at Covent Garden. She responded lightly to cheers from the auditorium. 'I will give each of you a sheep,' she called from her seat. 'It is the Karageorgevich way.'

The Yugoslav royal family is one of Europe's few native dynasties. It established, and lost, its crown through bloodshed, violence and intrigue. It was also to be implemented in the loss of other crowns as a result of Franz Ferdinand's assassination at Sarajevo by Serbian (Yugoslav) nationalists. Yet though it belongs to one of Europe's youngest countries, and is descended from a peasant, the Yugoslav royal family is today one of the most blue-blooded in the world and enjoys a closer relationship than most with the British monarchy. More than any other, the Karageorgevich dynasty gives the best illustration of a kingdom's rise and fall.

The founder, Karageorge – Black George – was a pig farmer who killed his mother by bonneting her with a hive of bees. In 1804 he turned his attention to the Turks and by acts of similar barbarity gained independence for Serbia, the nucleus of modern Yugoslavia. Unfortunately, Karageorge had made a few enemies on the way. One night he was murdered in his bed, and his severed head was despatched to Constantinople. Blame was laid at the door of a rival family, the Obrenoviches, who now came to power as kings. On 10 June 1903, an unusually hot and sultry day, the Obrenoviches had their come uppance. A group of officers stormed the royal palace in Belgrade and shot at everything in sight. The King and Queen scrambled from their bed and, scantily dressed, took refuge in a secret alcove. There they waited for two hours while infuriated soldiers searched the house and grounds. Unable to bear it any longer, the Queen opened the alcove's only window. Looking down at her flower bed, she immediately caught sight of the trusted commander of the Royal Guard. 'Your King is in danger,' she yelled. 'For God's sake to the rescue, to the rescue.' The faithful man raised his head, reached for his pistol and fired. As the Queen hurriedly closed the window, he grabbed an axe and rushed upstairs. The alcove was hacked open to reveal the royal couple in their nightshirts. Both were shot at point blank range. After mutilating the Queen and hurling her from the window, the assassins turned their attention to the King. He was still alive. As they carried him to the balcony, his hands clutched at the window pane, whereupon one of the soldiers unsheathed a sword and cut off his wrists. He was thrown with such force that on hitting the lawn, his right eye fell out of its socket. Their work done, the officers sat down and drank a toast to their new King, Black George's grandson, Peter Karageorge.

Peter I ascended the throne with a crown melted from one of Karageorge's cannons. 'My grandfather was of peasant stock,' he boasted, 'and I am prouder of that than of my throne.' Sensibly, he steered a less violent path. He translated Mill's *On Liberty* into Serbian and forced his eccentric and violent son, George, to renounce his rights after the boy had drowned his tutor in the Save, kicked a groom to death and taken pot-shots at the peasants from his window. Four days before Sarajevo, Peter appointed his younger son, Alexander, as Regent.

In November 1918 Serbia was amalgamated with chunks of Austria-Hungary, and made into the kingdom that was to be known as Yugoslavia.

Alexander, who succeeded as king in 1921, suffered the same fate as his ancestors. On a state visit to France in 1934, he was collected from the port ancestors. On a state visit to France in 1934, he was collected from the port at Marseilles in a car which struck its driver as 'more like a hearse than an automobile'. Ten minutes later a man in a brown suit bounded on to the running board. He was mistaken for a photographer, but the shots taken by Vlada the chauffeur, a Bulgarian in the pay of a Croatian terrorist organization, proved fatal. One of the bullets passed through Alexander's saluting hand. Unaware of what had happened the crowd continued to cry 'Vive le roi!' His last words were, 'Save Yugoslavia'.

Alexander's body was returned by sea. As it neared home a storm lashed the coast, unearthing the graves of several soldiers. It was rumoured that these fallen warriors had risen to greet their old commander. 'King Alexander was more popular assassinated than he was alive,' remarked Chips Channon. 'I wonder very much whether the Karageorgeviches are not doomed? . . . They all talk English amongst themselves, read *The Tatler*, barely understand Slavenian and dream of their next visit to London.'

At the time of Alexander's death his eleven-year-old son Peter was at Sandroyd preparatory school in Surrey, where he had thrown a fellow pupil over the bannisters for calling him 'a stinking little Balkan prince'. Protesting, 'I am too young to be a king,' he was sent back to Yugoslavia. Until he could accede on his eighteenth birthday, the government was to be placed under the control of a regent, his father's cousin Paul, father of Princess Elisabeth. Pressurized by both Russia and Germany, Paul was finally forced to sign a pact with the Nazis in the spring of 1940. At the instigation of the British, the Yugoslav army revolted and placed the seventeen-year-old Peter on the throne. Turning on the radio that morning, he heard a broadcast from a man claiming to be him. In a voice not unlike his own, the speaker called on his countrymen to rally round the throne. 'It is pure Ruritania,' was Chips Channon's reaction. Churchill was more enthusiastic. 'Yugoslavia has found its soul,' he told the House of Commons. Ten days later – the duration of Peter's reign – it lost its heart. Germany invaded. If Hitler's decision to postpone his attack on Russia was of vital help to the Allies, it precipitated the fall of the Karageorgevich dynasty.

Peter fled London where he formed a government in exile. Without the cohesion of ths monarchy, Yugoslav forces at home and abroad split into their traditonal factions. Soon they were not only fighting the Germans; they were fighting each other.

Churchill and Roosevelt lent vague support to Peter's resistance movement under General Mihailovic. Peter complained that it was not enough to equip a battalion. 'What do you expect them to fight with?' he demanded. 'Spades, pitchforks, fists?' His distress grew when the Allies switched their sympathies to Tito's partisans. Mihailovic had not been found trustworthy. 'I have no proof,' explained Churchill, 'but I am convinced he is collaborating.'

The rift was reflected in Peter's exiled government, which could not agree on anything. At Cambridge, where he was studying law, he grew even more restless and infuriated. 'If only I could do something. Oh God, if only I could do something.' He took up flying in the hope that Churchill would let him parachute into Yugoslavia and join up with Mihailovic. Churchill would not. After winning his RAF wings, he made plans to commandeer an old Halifax and crash-land in Serbia. Details of the mission leaked out and he was prevented from accompanying the flight. It was just as well. The plane was never heard of again.

In March 1944 Peter caused further friction among his cabinet, who held to a tradition that no Serx should marry in time of war. He married Princess Alexandra of Greece, like himself a great-great-grandchild of Queen Victoria. Alexandra was the daughter of King Alexander of Greece, who had died from a monkey bite. A photograph of her aged sixteen had impressed King Zog so much that he made plans for their future happiness. Unreliably advised thah she had a passion for oranges, Zog pressed his suit by shipping her crates of the world's finest Jaffas. He had been misinformed. 'I *loathed* oranges.'

Sixteen months after their marriage, at which George VI, known to them as Uncle Bertie, had served as best man, Alexandra went into labour on the second floor at Claridge's hotel in London.

During the war Claridge's, like the Ritz, was teeming with expatriated monarchs. A diplomat who rang for the King was asked by the receptionist 'Which one?' The manager's head was permanently inclined as he bowed them in and out of lifts and across the red carpet. George II of Greece was there, under the name of Mr Brown; so too were Queen Wilhelmina of the Netherlands, King Haakon of Norway, Grand Duchess Charlotte of Luxembourg – and Peter.

His royal suite was declared Yugoslav territory for the occasion of his son's birth on 17 July 1945; it was to be the boy's only experience of his national soil. Four months later, Tito, who had sent a delegation expressing the hope that the child would be a girl, abolished the monarchy, stopped the King's income and banned his family from returning. Events had disappointed Churchill's best hopes. As Channon said earlier, 'While helping Communists like Tito, he expects the King to be accepted on his shaky throne.' It had not happened. 'I did not betray you,' Churchill told Peter. 'I was betrayed.' Yet again the British had been instrumental in toppling a monarchy, as another commentator Liddell-Hart, was only too aware. 'The reponsibility for the consequent misery that has befallen the peoples [of] Yugoslavia and Greece lies heavily upon us – for losing all sense of military realities.' The misery was evident. Nearly two million Yugoslavs had died; 16 million were under Communist rule.

After 1945 Peter's life was, in the words of his son Alexander, 'pathetic, a disaster'. 'I want to be a King . . . I'm fit for nothing else,' he lamented. As long as he lived he would never stop fighting to return to his country; nor would he stop fighting to enable his son to return. 'And if I have to sell ice-cream or be a waiter, still I won't stop fighting.' He took his wife and child to America where he invested everything in a plastics factory and a shipping venture, both of which went broke. To pay for their hotel, he sold his evening dress, his Yugoslav Order and his wedding presents. Alexandra even contemplated working in a shop as a swim-suit salesgirl. Her wish for a domestic life conflicted with Peter's inability to forget he was a king. When America became too expensive, they returned to Europe, but they had no money. Hotels began to refuse them. Bailiffs impounded Alexandra's clothes. Suddenly she was tired of this 'empty masquerade'. Peter tried to make the young Alexander a ward of chancery. He saw other women, and he sued for divorce. 'You wanted me to be some sort of a country gentleman,' he raged, 'with nothing to do but play the role of British squire to my countrymen, potter about in the garden and always be at home.' She refused to divorce him. Eventually to settle their debts they sold the only thing they had left – their story. These autobiographies make painful reading. They are both apologies and curtain-calls. 'All my life,' wrote Alexandra, 'I have seen the neurotic results that exile has brought to political leaders. I know that *facts* cease to have meaning for them and there comes instead a political mania which makes them talk and think only of their return. As the years pass each scheme to achieve this becomes more improbable, but always, like gamblers, they are sure that *next* time it will be all right, *next* time they will win.' Fifteen years later, Peter died of alcohol poisoning in Denver.

A day before the Jerez sherry party I had been invited to lunch at Villa Manrique de la Condesa, a small, clean village, like starched linen, an hour's drive from Seville. Crown Prince Alexander was staying in a house behind the brick church which belonged to his father-in-law, Dom Pedro, and which had once belonged to the father of Queen Amélie of Portugal, the Count of Paris. It was here in 1972 that Alexander had married and it was to be here, in an upstairs room, that his twin sons were to be christened.

The square white house was built around an arcaded courtyard. It was covered by strips of cloth, to keep it cool by day and warm by night. In the arcades hung stags' horns, French battle prints and an oil-painting of a river donated by the Borough of Evesham. I walked through the courtyard, past four palm trees, and into the garden beyond. I found my host in blue trunks by the pool.

'If the US and Britain had given their full backing to my father, we would be a democracy today,' Alexander told me confidently. His accent was a mixture of public school and the army, well sauced with words like 'disaster', 'terrific', 'marvellous'. 'I'm not saying that we wouldn't have problems – all countries have problems – but it would have been very different and that much better for Europe.'

What did he think of his father's plans to join up with Mihailovic? He smiled. 'It would have been marvellous. The fairy-tale come true. The King coming down in his parachute. I just hope he would have landed all right. But it really would have given that little more backing to the guerilla forces who were fighting the Germans.' Did he regret that Peter never made the jump?

'I do, because I was a military man myself, and what – what great fun.'

It was as a lieutenant in the British army that he received news of his father's death. There was a move to make him King, 'a rather absurd move by some very loyal monarchists. As I said, King of what? I could not be King because there was no parliament to ratify the situation and above all, the country wasn't a democracy.' There were two other reasons. He was a member of the Queen's Royal Lancers and had become a naturalized British subject.

Alexander had joined the army in 1965, after an education at Gordonstoun – 'an awful place, miles from anywhere' – and Millfield, 'which was much better'. He served with a tank division in Germany and spent six months in County Tyrone. 'I was the first officer in the regiment to be

153

shot at.' In 1971, the year he was made Army ski champion, he announced his engagement to Princess Dona Maria of Orléans and Bragança, whom he had met in Portugal at a party given by the Countess of Paris, her aunt.

After they married, he resigned his commission and became an insurance executive. Today he works proudly for himself in Washington DC under the name of Alexander Karageorgevich, 'because it puts most people at ease.' He has not completely forgotten his inheritance.

'One's got to be a realist, but I think it's a going concern. I think it's a solution for uniting the country – all the different ethnic groups. Yugoslavia's in a terrible mess. It's the only country in the West which cannot enjoy the fruits of the West. There should be an alternative government and I would welcome a chance to be part of that, to see the democratic process return. I'm not a confirmed monarchist, but I do believe there is great admiration and support for my family there. At least they are mentioning me on Moscow Radio as the Naked Prince. The Prince of Nothing. What an honour. And in Yugoslavian papers, too, they lie about me forming a government in exile. But at least they mention me. There's some idea I should go back as a puppet and endorse the régime on television, but I wouldn't do that.'

For Alexander, exile is not too awful. As an insurance executive he knows the odds against becoming King and has restructured his life accordingly. As an insurance executive he also knows that odd things happen. Once a week he has a lesson in Serbo-Croat just in case they do.

At lunch, Dom Pedro explained how a metal plate in his leg always set off the security system at airports. He had just flown from Rio. The Brazilian Ambassador to Buenos Aires had told him that Galtieri was drunk when he made the decision to invade. Next day he didn't have the face to stop it. Alexander immediately began extolling the virtues of the British forces. 'Our troops are the best in the world', he exulted. 'Training, that's what it is. Those Gurkhas. Those Gurkhas.' He shook his head. He was particularly enthusiastic about Prince Andrew's role.

Over coffee, Alexander's wife wheeled in the twins: Alexander and Philip. 'They're quite extraordinary,' beamed their father. 'They have all the royal blood in Europe, but they're quite normal really.'

At the hotel Alfonso XIII in Seville, there was considerable commotion on the day of the christening. In the morning, Princess Elisabeth's companion had stomped up to the reception. 'How do I get upstairs?' he asked. 'The lifts don't work.' The receptionist looked at him blankly.

I made a suggestion. 'Use the staircase.'

He uttered a strangled cry, his eyes rolling. 'Staircase!' He turned back to the desk. 'How do I get upstairs?' he demanded again.

I escaped to the bar where guests were beginning to assemble before the trip to Villa Manrique. 'It's overpriced and awful,' the restaurateur was telling someone about one of Seville's better restaurants. A hand descended on my shoulder. It belonged to the pink-shirted Baron. In his other hand he held his familiar dossier. He insisted that I went with him round the corner. 'I'm sorry,' he explained, 'but that woman really hates me.' He indicated the demure Elisabeth who was busy soothing her irate friend. 'It's all to do with some photos in my book of Paul talking to Hitler. But one cannot rewrite history.' He sat down and went through his folio of photographs, stressing Yugoslavia's importance in the last war and the unimportance of dwelling on Peter's life 'after he was King'. He held up a coloured portrait of Alexander's father. 'I mean something like this is a beautiful thing.' Then he very kindly gave me a copy of his book. I was instructed to hide it, just in case 'that woman' saw.

That afternoon Dom Pedro exchanged his khaki shorts for a grey suit and put his straw hat on an antler in the hall. At his front door he greeted friends and relations who had come from all over Europe for the christening of his grandsons. Late arrivals included his two sisters, the Countess of Paris and Princess Teresa; the principal godparent, King Constantine of Greece and his wife. And last of all, Constantine's brother-in-law, the star of the show.

Escorted by two police cars, a dark armour-plated limousine roared up the cobbled drive. The driver, dressed in a white suit, was King Juan Carlos of Spain.

For fourty-four years there was no reign in Spain. In 1931 the dashing Alfonso XIII had been ousted by a referendum. 'I felt like a man calling on an old friend and finding him dead.'

He had, in a sense, been prepared. 'No king can qualify for his job unless prepared to endure the ingratitude of his people.' His people had indeed been ungrateful. Alfonso, who had been born posthumously and become King at the moment of his birth, was to escape with a number of assassination attempts exceeded only by Nicholas II. 'I prefer revolvers to bombs, was a verdict he reached at an early age. On his wedding day the anarchist Mateo Morrales had waved a bulky bouquet from a fourth-storey balcony on the Calle Major, and then thrown it at the royal carriage. The bouquet concealed a bomb which killed twenty-eight men, wounded scores more and splattered the blood of men and horses over the Queen's bridal gown.

On hearing the results of the referendum nearly thirty years after, Alfonso's reaction was that of any monarch. 'It is better to go into exile than to be responsible for bloodshed.' He made his way to the Hotel Savoy, Fontainebleau. Here in April 1814 Napoleon had given his farewell speech to the old guard before abdicating in favour of Louis XVIII. Over a century later, Alfonso had no intention of doing any such thing. 'I have not abdicated as yet. Do not forget it!' he insisted from a dining salon which had formerly been the billiard room. When the editor of a news-paper offered him $10,000 to write 1000 words, Alfonso's humorous eyes lit up. 'He wanted a thousand words when there is just one worthwhile word left in my vocabulary, but that word is not for sale. Spain.'

While he spent his last years playing bridge at the Grand Hotel in Rome, Spain was recovering from civil war under the grip of General Franco, that champion against Communism. Alfonso's son and heir, the liberal Don Juan, Count of Barcelona, served six years in the Royal Navy before settling in Portugal to await the call. It would come, he was convinced. sure enough, in 1947 Spain was declared a monarchy. Using that old royalist, Ricardo Espirito Santo, to arrange a get-together with Don Juan, Franco invited him aboard his yacht in the Bay of Biscay. It was, in keeping with the location, a stormy meeting. They agreed on one thing only: to bring up Don Juan's eldest son in Spain. In 1948 the ten-year-old boy left his home in Rua Inglaterra, Estoril, and caught a train across the border. Under Franco's watchful eye, he received an education in the three armed services and in 1969, against his father's wishes, he accepted the throne – to which he would accede on Franco's death.

In November 1975 he was duly elected King Juan Carlos I. Though he was known on his accession as Juan Carlos el Breve, the Brief, the security of his tenure is of little moment to his dispossessed relatives. More important to them is the fact that a republic has given way to a monarchy. They were in need of such encouragement.

In the upstairs room kings and queens, pretenders and claimants tapped each other on the shoulder, turned and shook hands, and stood quietly for the ceremony to begin. A Serbian bishop, dressed in a gold mitre and embroidered robes, lit the candles with a cigarette lighter. One by one, as Alexander's ADC swung an incense burner chanting 'Lord have mercy on us', the twins were carried in and placed in the hands of their respective godparents. They screamed so much that at one point King Juan Carlos turned round to Countess of Paris and muttered something about a bullfight. King Constantine looked down uncomfortably at the bundle in his arms and tried to soothe it. Then he walked to the central table where the bishop dunked the baby in a bowl of water. This was the cause of more howling.

One month later, King Constantine's more famous godson, Prince William of England, was to make the same noise, at his christening. On this early evening in Spain, I began to wonder whether the incessant howls were just the reaction of healthy boys or perhaps the prescient recognition of what it meant to carry the blood – and the burden – of most of the royal families in Europe.

Afterwards, while the family assembled in the garden for a photograph, I walked down the stairs and into the courtyard. Beside two barrels of sherry, donated by Gonzalez-Byass, I saw the Baron in conversation with a guest. The man had a dull smile on his face. 'Ah,' said the Baron. 'I was telling him about the portrait of Isabel II upstairs.' In one of the arcades, the security men had lit up and were drinking liberally from a tray of beer. The garden party began trickling back. The Countess of Paris's daughter was eulogizing her mother. 'She's a saint,' she said. Alexander came up in panic. His oldest son, Peter, had gone missing during the christening. He had been discovered turning on all the taps in the house. 'Do come and see us in Washington,' he urged.

In the mêlée, I caught sight of Princess Elisabeth, shadowed by her companion. Every now and then he tried to say something, but she seemed happier talking with the Queen of Spain. The scene brought to mind a story about Elisabeth's mother, Princess Olga. In London during the last war, long after the fall of Yugoslavia, she was dining with some friends at Ciro's. Suddenly the restaurant fell silent. The lull was broken by a thick foreign accent as Olga declared for all to hear: 'So boring not to reign.'

Bibliography

General Books

Bocca, Geoffrey, *The Uneasy Heads*, Weidenfeld & Nicolson, 1959
Burke's Royal Families of the World, vol.I: 'Europe and Latin America', ed. Hugh Montgomery-Massingberd, Burke's Peerage, 1977
Curley, Walter J.P., *Monarchs in Waiting*, Hutchinson, 1975
Ernst, Dr Otto, *Kings in Exile*, Jarrolds, 1933
Fenyvesi, Charles, *Royalty in Exile*, Robson Books, 1981
Figgis, J.N., *The Divine Right of Kings*, Cambridge University Press, 1922
Finestone, Jeffrey, *The Last Courts of Europe*, J.M. Dent, 1981
Hamilton, Gerald, *Blood Royal*, Anthony Gibbs & Phillips, 1964
Judd, Denis, *Eclipse of Kings: European Monarchies in the Twentieth Century*, Macdonald and Jane's, 1976
Murray-Brown, Jeremy (ed.), *The Monarchy and its Future*, Allen & Unwin, 1969
Petrie, Sir Charles, *Monarchy in the Twentieth Century*, Andrew Dakers, 1952
Pine, L.G., *The Twilight of Monarchy*, Burke's Peerage, 1958
Vare, Daniel, *Twilight of the Kings*, John Murray, 1948
Walzer, Michael, *Regicide and Revolution*, Cambridge University Press, 1974

1 Dear Old Twick

Bleach, Vincent, *Charles X of France*, Pruett, Colorado, 1971
Corpechot, Lucien, *Memories of Queen Amélie of Portugal*, Eveleigh Nash, 1915
Cripps, F.H., *Life's a Gamble*, Odhams Press, 1957
de Bragança-Cunha, V., *Eight Centuries of Portuguese Monarchy*, Swift, 1911
    Revolutionary Portugal 1910-36, James Clarke, 1938

Gribble, F., *The Royal House of Portugal*, Eveleigh Nash, 1915
Guest, Ivor, *Napoleon III in England*, British Technical and General Press, 1952
Hardinge, C.H., *Old Diplomacy*, John Murray, 1947
Howarth, T., *Citizen King*, Eyre & Spottiswoode, 1961
Memoirs of HRH Prince Chistopher of Greece, Hurst & Blackett, 1938
Rheinhardt, E., *Napoleon and Eugénie*, Hutchinson, 1932
Ridley, Jasper, *Napoleon III and Eugénie*, Constable, 1979
Sanders, M., *Louis XVIII*, Hutchinson, 1910
Seward, Desmond, *The Bourbon Kings of France*, Constable, 1976
Stenger, G., *The Return of Louis XVIII*, Heinemann, 1909
Weiner, Margery, *The French Exiles 1789-1815*, John Murray, 1960

2 'Gone with the Windsors'
Birkenhead, Lord, *Walter Monckton*, Weidenfeld & Nicolson, 1969
Bloch, Michael, *The Duke of Windsor's War*, Weidenfeld & Nicolson, 1982
Bocca, Geoffrey, *The Life and Death of Sir Harry Oakes*, Weidenfeld & Nicolson, 1959
Bryan, J. and Murphy, Charles J.V., *The Windsor Story*, Granada, 1979
By Safe Hand: The Wartime Letters of David and Sybil Eccles, Bodley Head, 1983
Chips: the Diaries of Sir Henry Channon 1934-53, ed. R.R. James, Weidenfeld & Nicolson, 1967
Gilbert, Martin, *Churchill's Finest Hour*, Heinemann, 1983
Greenwall, Harry, *Our Oldest Ally*, W.H. Allen, 1943
Hoare, Sir Samuel, *Nine Troubled Years*, Collins, 1954
Macaulay, Rose, *They Went to Portugal*, Jonathan Cape, 1946
Martin, Ralph, C., *The Woman He Loved*, W.H. Allen, 1974
Selby, Sir Walford, *Diplomatic Twilight*, John Murray, 1953

3 King Carol and Madame Lupescu
Cartland, Barbara, *The Scandalous Life of King Carol*, Corgi, 1974
Easterman, A.L., *King Carol, Hitler, Lupescu*, Victor Gollancz, 1942
Lees-Milne, James, *Harold Nicolson, A Biography*, Chatto & Windus, 1981
Moats, Alice Leone, *Lupescu*, Henry Holt, New York, 1955
Romania, Marie, Queen of, *The Story of my Life* (3 vols), Cassell, 1934–5
von der Hoven, Baroness Helena, *King Carol of Romania*, Hutchinson, 1940

4 The May King
Barzini, Luigi, *From Caesar to the Mafia*, Hamish Hamilton, 1971
Castellani, Aldo, *Microbes, Men and Monarchs*, Victor Gollancz, 1960
Collier, Richard, *Duce*, Collins, 1971
Katz, Robert, *The Fall of the House of Savoy*, Allen & Unwin, 1971
Lucifero, Falcone (ed.), *Il Re Dall'Esilio*, Silvio Mursia, Milan, 1978
Murphy, R., *Diplomat Among Warriors*, Collins, 1964
Robertson, Alexander, *Victor Emmanuel III*, Allen & Unwin, 1925

5 The French Claimant
de Gaulle, Charles, *Memoirs of Hope*, Weidenfeld & Nicolson, 1971
Osgood, Samuel M., *French Royalism under the Third and Fourth Republics*,
    Martinus Nijhoff, The Hague, 1960
Paris, Henri, Comte de, *Memoires d'Exil et de Combats*, Atelier Marcel
    Jullian, Paris, 1979
Paris, Isabelle, Comtesse de, *Tout m'est Bonheur*, Robert Laffont, Paris,
    1978
Tournoux, J.R., *La Tragédie du Général*, Plon, Paris, 1967

6 Sebastianismo
Ingram, J.H., *Claimants to Royalty*, David Bogue, 1882

7 Mr Europe
De Harding, Bertita Leonarz, *Imperial Twilight: The Story of Karl and Zita
    of Hungary*, Harrap, 1940
Horthy, Admiral Nicholas, *Memoirs*, Hutchinson, 1956
Ryan, Nellie, *My Years at the Austrian Court*, Bodley Head, 1918
Shepherd, Gordon Brook, *The Last Habsburg*, Weidenfeld & Nicolson,
    1968
Vasari, Emilio, *Dr Otto von Habsburg*, Verlag Herold, Wien/Munchen,
    1972
Vivian, Herbert, *The Life of the Emperor Charles of Austria*, Grayson &
    Grayson, 1932
von Habsburg, Otto, *The Social Order of Tomorrow*, Oswald Wolff, 1958

8 Dr Ferdinand
Bentinck, Lady Norah, *The Ex-Kaiser in Exile*, Hodder & Stoughton,
    1921

Cowles, V., *The Kaiser*, Collins, 1963

Henry, W., *The Soldier Kings*, J.M. Dent, 1971

The Kaiser's Daughter: Memoirs of HRH Viktoria Luise, Duchess of Brunswick and Lüneburg, ed. Robert Vacha, W.H. Allen, 1977

Jonas, K., *Life of Crown Prince William*, Routledge Kegan Paul, 1961

Palmer, Alan, *The Kaiser: Warlord of the Second Reich*, Scribner's, New York, 1978 and Weidenfeld & Nicolson, 1978

Prussia, Louis Ferdinand, Prince of, *The Rebel Prince*, Henry Regnery, 1952

Waters, Brigadier-General W., *Potsdam and Doorn*, John Murray, 1935

X.7, *The Return of Kings*, Eveleigh Nash, 1925

9 Imperial Mist

Cowles, V., *The Romanovs*, Collins, 1971

Kurth, Peter, *Anastasia: The Riddle of Anna Anderson*, Jonathan Cape, 1983

Massie, R.K., *Nicholas and Alexandra*, Victor Gollancz, 1968

Summers, A. and Mangold, T., *The File on the Tsar*, Victor Gollancz, 1976

Youssoupoff, Felix, *Lost Splendour*, Jonathan Cape, 1953

Walsh, W.T., *Our Lady of Fátima*, Macmillan, 1949

10 How to be a King

Araucanie, Philippe Prince d', *Histoire du Royaume d'Araucanie*, SFA, Paris, 1979

Bolitho, Hector, *James Lyle Mackay, First Earl of Inchcape*, John Murray, 1938

Brooke, Sylvia, *Queen of the Headhunters*, Sidgwick & Jackson, 1970

Chatwin, Bruce, *In Patagonia*, Jonathan Cape, 1977

Crisswell, Colin, *Rajah Charles Brooke: Monarch of all he Surveyed*, Oxford University Press, 1978

des Vergnes, André, *Antoine de Tounens*, La Rochelle, 1979

Fry, C.B., *Life Worth Living*, Eyre & Spottiswoode, 1939

Hahn, Emily, *James Brooke of Sarawak*, Arthur Barker, 1953

Luke, Sir Harry, *In the Margin of History*, Dickson Lovat, 1933

Montgomery-Massingberd, Hugh and Watkin, David, *The London Ritz*, Aurum Press, 1980

Pringle, R., *Rajahs and Rebels*, Macmillan, 1970

Runcieman, Steven, *The White Rajahs*, Cambridge University Press, 1960

Sarawak, Ranee of, *The Three White Rajahs*, Cassell, 1939
Swire, J. W., *Albania. The Rise of a Kingdom*, Robert Hale, 1929
   King Zog's Albania, Robert Hale, 1937

11 The Pretenders

Aronson, Theo, *Kings over the Water*, Cassell, 1979
Domela, Harry, *A Sham Prince*, Hutchinson, 1927
A Legitimist Kalendar 1895, ed. Marquis de Ruvigny and Raineval, Henry & Co., 1894
Lister, Roma, *Reminiscences Social and Political*, Hutchinson, 1926
Nicolson, Harold, *George V*, Constable, 1952
Rose, Kenneth, *George V*, Weidenfeld & Nicolson, 1983
Scott, Sir Walter, *Redgauntlet*, J.M. Dent, 1967

12 Till Their Kingdoms Come

Graham, S., *Alexander of Yugoslavia*, Cassell, 1938
Jukic, Ilija, *The Fall of Yugoslavia*, Harcourt Brace Jovanvich, New York, 1974
A Kings Heritage. The Memoirs of King Peter II of Yugoslavia, Cassell, 1955
Mijatovich, Chedomille, *A Royal Tragedy*, Eveleigh Nash, 1906
Petrie, Sir Charles, *Alfonso XIII and his Age*, Chapman & Hall, 1963
Russia, Alexander, Grand Duke of, *Twilight of Royalty*, Ray Long & Richard R. Smith, New York, 1932
Yugoslavia, Queen Alexandra of, *For a King's Love*, Odhams Press, 1956

Periodicals

The Monarchist, Journal of the Monarchist League
The Orléans Family in Twickenham 1800-92, Twickenham Local History Society
Otto of Austria: Monarchy in the Atomic Age, Monarchist Press Association
Yugoslavia's Royal Dynasty, Monarchist Press Association

Index

Index